Flight 777

By the same author

I Saw the World - Poems of Walther von der Vogelweide set into English
Domesday Village
Chief of Intelligence
The Unknown Courier
Flight 777
Colonel Henri's Story, by Hugo Bleicher and Ian Colvin
The Rise and Fall of Moise Tshombe
Vansittart in Office
The Chamberlain Cabinet

Would he, so developed, breathe and move, be warm
To an optic music, stride from the cul-de-sac
Of cradling ocean, heroic as in a fable,
And around my shoulder place his unforgotten arm.

Ronald Howard

Flight 777

The Mystery of Leslie Howard

Ian Colvin

Pen & Sword
AVIATION

First published in Great Britain in 1957
Reprinted in this format in 2013 by
Pen & Sword Aviation
an imprint of
Pen & Sword Books Ltd
47 Church Street
Barnsley
South Yorkshire S70 2AS

New editorial material and arrangement © Clare Colvin and
Andrew Colvin, 2013
Copyright © Ian Colvin, 1957 and 2013

ISBN 978-1-78159-016-4

A CIP catalogue entry for this book is available from the British Library.

Typeset in Ehrhardt MT by
Mac Style, Driffield, East Yorkshire

Printed and bound in the UK by CPI Group (UK) Ltd, Croydon, CRO 4YY

Pen & Sword Books Ltd includes the Imprints of Pen & Sword Aviation,
Pen & Sword Family History, Pen & Sword Maritime, Pen & Sword Military,
Wharncliffe Local History, Pen & Sword Select, Pen & Sword Military Classics,
Leo Cooper, The Praetorian Press, Remember When, Seaforth Publishing
and Frontline Publishing.

For a complete list of Pen & Sword titles please contact
PEN & SWORD BOOKS LIMITED
47 Church Street, Barnsley, South Yorkshire, S70 2AS, England
E-mail: enquiries@pen-and-sword.co.uk
Website: www.pen-and-sword.co.uk

Contents

Illustrations

The author Ian Colvin shortly after joining the Royal Marines, 1942
An early Douglas DC-3 in flight
An exhibition catalogue by sculptor Oscar Nemon
Leslie Howard with his likeness, and Oscar Nemon
Sculpture by Oscar Nemon of Violette Cunnington
Leslie with Violette in 'Pimpernel Smith'
A KLM DC-3 crew at Whitchurch
Engbertus Rosevink, flight engineer on Flight 777
Loading a life-raft on to a KLM Douglas DC-3
A victorious Luftwaffe aircrew at Meriquac airfield
Junkers Ju88 aircrew members relaxing in 1943
Leslie Howard arriving for the film premiere of 'Pygmalion'
Frank Foley, Berlin Head of MI6 in 1939
Winston Churchill and General James Doolittle study air reconnaissance
    photographs
A man of many parts
Dirk Parmentier, veteran K.L.M. pilot The doomed airliner, *Ibis*
Quirinus Tepas Alfred Chenhalls
Baron Oswald Hoyningen-Huene
Lisbon Sir Ronald Campbell
Leslie Howard as Romeo in 'Romeo and Juliet' (1936)
As R.J. Mitchell, in 'The First of the Few'
Wilfrid Berthold Israel
Ivan Sharp
Alfred Chenhalls
Leslie Howard at a picnic beach near Lisbon on the day before he was killed
Leslie Howard and Alfred Chenhalls meet Press correspondents
Field Marshal Sperrle
One of the Luftwaffe units of Group K.G. 40
Engbertus Rosevink
Captain D. de Koning
Captain Theo Verhoeven
Leslie Howard poses in happy mood with Conchita Montenegro
Leslie Howard and Alfred Chenhalls at one of the last cocktail parties in Lisbon

For permission to reproduce photographs in this book the publishers are indebted to: Associated Press; Exclusive News Agency; Imperial War Museum; International Services Ltd.; Keystone Press Agency; K.L.M.; Ministry of Information; National Film Archive; O Seculo, Lisbon; Placar Nacional, Lisbon; Portuguese Tourist Office; Bonneville, Bergen NH/Jan Hagens, Heiloo, Londen Of Berlijn; the Nemon Estate; Ben Rosevink; Michael Smith.

Introduction to the 2012 Edition

Clare Colvin

Ian Colvin's lifelong interest in Britain's Secret Intelligence battles against the Nazis began when he worked as a journalist for the *News Chronicle* in Berlin during 1938–39. He came into contact with members of the German undercover opposition to Hitler, and stepped over the line between reporting events and taking part in them. Winston Churchill wrote in *The Gathering Storm*:

> Ian Colvin delved deeply into German affairs and maintained contacts of a most secret nature with some of the important German Generals and also with independent men of character and quality who saw in the Hitler Movement the approaching ruin of their fatherland.

Colvin helped to arrange a clandestine visit to London by one of the anti-Hitler elements, Ewald von Kleist-Schmenzin, with the aim of influencing the British Government to take a firm stand against Hitler's threatened invasion of Czechoslovakia. Then came the 1938 Munich Agreement, with Chamberlain's naive reliance on a piece of paper promising 'peace for our time', and the moment to topple Hitler was lost. The following year Colvin himself flew to London and his arguments persuaded the Cabinet to give a guarantee to Poland. Hitler, already contemptuous of Chamberlain's weakness and the dilatory manner in which the Guarantee was approved, invaded Poland. On 3 September 1939 Britain declared war against Germany.

Although the British Ambassador in Berlin, Sir Nevile Henderson, toed the Government line on appeasement, there were others in the Embassy and Consulate who did not. One, whom Colvin knew, was Frank Foley. His job as Passport Control Officer was a cover for his role as MI6 head of station in the German capital. At the 1961 trial of Adolf Eichmann, Foley was described as the 'Scarlet Pimpernel' who had risked his own life to save Jews threatened with death by the Nazis. It was only in the excellent biography *Foley – The Spy who Saved 10,000 Jews* by Michael Smith that the full extent of his heroism was revealed.

Foley was the sort of unobtrusive man on whom a fictional spy, like John Le Carré's George Smiley, could have been modelled, rather than Ian Fleming's flamboyant James Bond. A civil servant working in Passport Control described him as adopting the role of being "rather a feckless, awfully nice chap, but not really somebody you could take seriously. You would never have dreamt".

The twenty-six-year-old Colvin had the utmost regard for this courageous man, and they kept in touch after the war. In fact, Colvin was married to Moira Muntz, whom he had met when she was working as one of Foley's secretaries in Passport Control. Foley was one of Colvin's sources for his book about Admiral Canaris, *Chief of Intelligence*, published in 1951. Foley was also the anonymous 'Hush Man' mentioned as briefing Colvin on Operation MINCEMEAT, the subject of Colvin's second book on wartime espionage, *The Unknown Courier* (re-published by Faber Finds).

With *Flight 777* (published in 1957), which examines the shooting down during a flight from Lisbon to Bristol of the aircraft on which two leading anti-Nazis, Leslie Howard and Wilfrid Israel, were travelling – things become even more 'Hush'. Howard, as a celebrated film actor/director, and Israel, in his work rescuing

Jewish youths from the Nazis, had both earned the soubriquet 'Scarlet Pimpernel'.

Howard had modestly told Israel, when they met in Madrid during his lecture tour, that he had only acted the role, whereas Israel had lived it, but the truth was rather more complex. The actor had returned to Britain from Hollywood at the start of the war, sacrificing the continuance of royalties from *Gone with the Wind*, with a mission to direct films designed to bolster national morale. The effectiveness of the films *Pimpernel Smith*, about freeing concentration camp prisoners in pre-war Nazi Germany, and *The First of the Few*, about the designer of the Spitfire, had infuriated Dr Goebbels, German Minister for Propaganda.

Leslie Howard's lecture tour to Spain and Portugal in late May 1943 was sufficiently sensitive to involve correspondence with Anthony Eden, the Foreign Secretary, after Howard had expressed reluctance to go ahead with the Spanish part of the tour. Eden wrote to him on 20 April 1943 that it was "very important just now to fly the British flag in Spain and to give encouragement to our many friends there, who are to be found in all classes".

Theatricals, such as Noel Coward and Laurence Olivier, had been recruited by the Security Service to target American opinion during the years of United States neutrality. Howard was visiting Spain at a time when General Franco was being urged by Hitler to abandon his neutral stance and join the Axis. Howard had first met Winston Churchill around 1937 during several informal talks on plans to film the story of Lawrence of Arabia. His theatre and film agent Alfred Chenhalls's sister Joan was a member of MI5. During wartime, when travel was restricted, it would be reasonable for the Government to expect famous figures to use their influence in aiding the war effort. Howard, as the son of a Jewish Hungarian immigrant, Ferdinand

Steiner, and a partly Jewish mother, was as aware as anyone of the consequences of the Iberian Peninsula abandoning its neutrality for the Axis side.

In *Flight 777*, however, there is a third man also known as a 'Scarlet Pimpernel', who remains elusively in the shadows. In 1943 Frank Foley was part of British Intelligence's Twenty Committee, which dealt in the world of double-agents and double-bluff. A few selected members of the Committee would have known about the highly secret *Ultra* intelligence that was used to decode the Germans' Enigma messages, and undoubtedly shortened the war. Much of Foley's work was based on German espionage activities in Spain and Portugal, from where the Abwehr was attempting to infiltrate its agents into Britain. What Colvin's book doesn't mention, although he was aware of the fact, is that Foley was actually in Portugal at the same time as Leslie Howard, and was fortunate not to be on the flight.

There has been much speculation over the last minute decision by Leslie Howard and his agent, Alfred Chenhalls, to travel on 1 June, rather than a day later. Whether Howard's hasty decision was due to nerves about German agents who had been watching him or for personal reasons is not known, but the flight was full when they changed their plans. The only way to get on to it was by pulling VIP status and have others bumped off the plane. In Michael Smith's *Foley*, a niece of Foley tells a story which she must have heard from her Uncle Frank that, while he was waiting at Lisbon airport to board the flight to Bristol, he met Gordon Maclean, Inspector General of His Majesty's Consulates, who asked if they could change places as Leslie Howard was his wife's favourite actor and he wanted to get his autograph. According to this account, Foley agreed, and shortly before ten o'clock the DC-3, with thirteen passengers and four crew on board, took off. A few hours later it was shot down over the Bay of Biscay by German fighter aircraft, with the loss of all on board.

This is very different from Colvin's version of events, which states that Howard and Chenhalls had claimed priority to travel around 5pm on the previous day. The secretary to the air attaché of the British Embassy in Lisbon, according to Colvin, then rang the English College, a recusant seminary for secular priests, and spoke to 'Father Holmes', asking to hold him over until Wednesday 2 June. Ronald Howard's book *In Search of My Father* gives yet another sequence of events – that a priest already on board the aircraft had disembarked on being called urgently to the telephone and did not return.

A travelling priest seems to have cropped up on another of the Bristol–Lisbon flights. Of the four DC-3s that the Dutch crew flew, the *Ibis* – in which the ex-KLM men had escaped from Schiphol airport when the Nazis invaded Holland – had already been attacked twice by German fighters on the Lisbon run, once in November 1942, when it was carrying twelve passengers, and again in April 1943, when it flew from Bristol with only three passengers – a Swiss courier with diplomatic bags, a businessman and a priest. In that attack over the Bay of Biscay it escaped with damage to one wing. The third time, on 1 June 1943, was fatal for the *Ibis* and those aboard.

The story of Flight 777, indeed, could be regarded less as a 'Whodunit?' than a 'Who was the target?' Of the thirteen passengers there were several whom the Germans would have liked to have seen dead, the most conspicuous amongst them being Leslie Howard. Wilfrid Israel was another and there was also Ivan Sharp, the mining expert whose buying up of tungsten at inflated prices for the British

Government was hampering the German armaments industry. Then there was the suggestion, voiced by Churchill, who had been in Algiers at the time after visiting Washington in May 1943, that Howard's agent, the tubby, cigar-smoking Alfred Chenhalls, had been mistaken for the Prime Minister. Certainly, the Luftwaffe was on high alert, their spies desperately chasing rumours as to which route would be used to fly Churchill back to England.

Fifty-six years after it was first published, Colvin's story of the wartime tragedy retains its immediacy and almost filmic quality. The re-publication of *Flight 777* includes added footnotes by his son Andrew Colvin that clarify some of the accounts and answer intriguing questions, such as the likely identity of the glamorous double agent, Countess Miranda, who became involved with Howard during his tour of the Iberian Peninsula. We should like to thank James Oglethorpe for his invaluable help in locating relevant archival documents. The new material throws light on Howard's connections with British Intelligence and his personal life, drawing on files from the National Archives that have only become available in recent years. It also examines the question as to whether British Intelligence knew beforehand that Flight 777 would be a likely target for attack. This is a debate that continues today among students of the shadowy world of espionage.

Clare Colvin
April 2012

Foreword

The data on which this book is written has been collected over a number of years. Thanks to documents discovered in the archives of the Royal Dutch Airlines, to the assistance of the official historians and pilots of BOAC, KLM and the *Luftwaffe* it is possible to present this as a documentary work.

In all cases where living persons are quoted, the conversations are based on their own narrative, with the exception of foreign spies and Allied counter-espionage agents figuring in the story, whose roles have been reconstructed on reliable evidence.

Similarly, dialogues between the dead have been drawn out of the subject itself. I have given much study to each character and the circumstances in which they entered the story, and trust that the reader will understand my spanning certain gaps, which could not otherwise be bridged, by conjuring up direct speech. Before depicting the scene in which Leslie Howard decides to go to Europe, I immersed myself in newspaper interviews with him and in articles which he wrote for the *Sunday Chronicle,* in order to recapture his way of speaking; the scene is otherwise imaginary but, I think, not unlike him.

I have drawn here and there on imagination, but where there has been an available witness, his memory has guided me. In certain cases I have been able to describe scenes of twelve and fifteen years ago with photographic exactitude, and that has simply been because I have had actual photographs available to study. The tie that Leslie Howard wore at a Lisbon cocktail party, the book that he marked, the itinerary and its dates are all genuine stage properties, and I do not think that I have been incautious either in my portrayal of the emotions and behaviour of my characters. The coincidental and the near supernatural which seem to run through this story, like a grey skein, have been thoroughly tested. The thirteen at table, the gipsy sayings, the forecast of the spiritualist are vouched for. The character described as the Countess Miranda is a synthesis of various qualities exhibited by known enemy spies. More than one German woman agent was instructed to observe and report on Leslie Howard during his last visit to the Peninsula.

It remains for me to thank those who have assisted me in the gathering of my material: the Royal Dutch Airlines, British Overseas Airways, the Services historians, the British Council. I must especially mention Professor Walter Starkie, Mr George West, Mr A. E. Johnson, Mr F. A. M. Wilbers, Mr John Bradshaw, British Consul in Lisbon, Mr Freddie Gilman of BOAC, Mr Isidoro Balbuena, Baron Oswald Hoyningen-Huene, Wing Commander J. Schuldam-Schreiber, Mr Ronald Howard, Mr Arthur Howard, Miss Irene Howard, Anatole de Grunwald, and Mr Oskar Nemon, the sculptor. My thanks are also due to Mrs Sylvia Latham, Miss Adrienne Harvey, Mrs Sheila Baklanova and, as ever, to Frank Betts I owe my particular gratitude.

Chapter 1

Mystery of an Aircraft

On 1 June 1943 a civil airliner on the Lisbon to England route was shot down over the Bay of Biscay. A small incident, no doubt, in the vast tragedies of the Second World War, but it happened during a lull between campaigns. The war in North Africa was over, the invasion of Sicily had not yet begun, the bombing of the Ruhr was proceeding according to plan, and there were only small-scale operations reported from Burma and South-East Asia. So the incident was reported at considerable length.

The circumstances, too, made it a poignant loss for the British public: for among the thirteen passengers was Leslie Howard, the actor and film star.

First, angry questions were asked in Parliament about the dangers of daylight flying on the Lisbon route. Then reports began to circulate that showed some mystery about the incident. It has remained a mystery ever since.

Later in 1943 passengers arriving in London from Lisbon said guardedly:

"There was something curious about that aircraft."

Of course, Leslie Howard was on board. A man was also on board who resembled Churchill and smoked a cigar. Moreover, none of the other aircraft that daily flew this route by daylight had, according to the Air Ministry, been involved in any such incident.

This case became a mystery of the air such as that of the *Marie Celeste* on the seas. It was long remembered for the sudden shock that it gave to millions of people as the London newsbills read, "Leslie Howard shot down".

Nobody had found a satisfactory explanation for it ten years later, when I began this investigation. Everybody seemed to know something about those who had been on board, or had heard of somebody who was taken off at the last moment, or had some notion as to why it was shot down. One theory was that the Germans had believed Churchill to be on board. Another was that they had wished to settle a score with Leslie Howard for his wartime propaganda work.

These were the two versions that I have heard most often.

A list of the thirteen passengers, all of whom lost their lives, was quickly published. At first sight there was no other notable person on board. The crew of four were all Dutchmen and the plane was one of the Royal Dutch airliners, lent on charter to BOAC. Yet the speculation went on.

For there was something unusual about the Lisbon route and the aircraft that flew it. Day after day since 1940 the airliners that served London and Lisbon led a charmed existence. They plied from England without interference. It was said that a secret understanding had been reached between Great Britain and Germany through the protecting power for this civil airline to continue unmolested, as it carried prisoner-of-war mail, neutral diplomats, and diplomatic bags. It was even said that it was of considerable interest to the Germans not to interrupt the Lisbon route from England, because it took in their spies and brought out the British newspapers – a mine of information to the German Intelligence Service. Why, then, should this aircraft have been shot down?

Despite all conjecture at the time, the mystery remained. The war moved into other stages. The operations in Normandy a year later cleared the whole of France and the Biscay area of enemy aircraft. A year after that the Luftwaffe had ceased to exist. The victors sorted the prisoners in the cages, and sifted the captured documents.

The Allies had first to deal with major war crimes. The Field Marshals, the Admirals and Air Generals, and the Cabinet Ministers were tried for blind obedience to their Führer and carrying total war to its ultimate conclusion. Then the lesser cases were heard, and particularly the crimes against civilians. I supposed that we should know eventually how and why Leslie Howard and his companions met death that day over the Bay of Biscay; for if ever an act of war merited a war-crimes trial, this seemed to be it. The Wehrmacht culprits, the SS colonels, the Security Service men, and the German diplomats came up for trial, but there was never any mention in the indictments of the civilian plane that was callously shot down on the Lisbon route. There was official silence, no move, no explanation – a mystery within a mystery. Had the Germans, then, covered their tracks so well?

This puzzled me as I travelled about Germany after the war reporting war-crimes trials.[1] Somewhere among the lorry-loads of captured war archives there *must* be a clue to it all.

It was not easy to sift the human flotsam of the Third Reich. The Luftwaffe was scattered, some of its officers were in hiding and have evaded questioning to this day. We journalists had no access to internment camps, and Allied decrees had abolished any kind of regimental club or ex-servicemen's associations. There was no means then of getting in touch with members of disbanded units, even if those units could be identified.

So it was 1950 before anything notable was added to the unfinished story of the aircraft that was lost on the Lisbon route. Then Sir Winston Churchill, in his memoirs, going in giant strides again over the battlefields, paused to relate the accepted version.

In June 1943 the Prime Minister was about to fly home from North Africa, but his route and time of departure were kept a strict secret. In that unlucky airliner there had been a British passenger who resembled the Prime Minister and smoked cigars. German agents in Portugal had seen him and reported their suspicions: the airliner had been intercepted and shot down.

In *The Hinge of Fate* Sir Winston told of his own visit to Washington in May 1943, and how he had proceeded to Algiers to survey the Mediterranean theatre of operations.

Eden and I flew home together from Gibraltar. As my presence in North Africa had been fully reported, the Germans were exceptionally vigilant and this led to a tragedy which much distressed me.

The regular commercial aircraft was about to start from the Lisbon airfield when a thickset man smoking a cigar walked up and was thought to be a passenger on it. The German agents therefore signalled that I was on board. Although these neutral passenger planes plied unmolested for many months between Portugal and England and had carried only civilian traffic, a German war plane was instantly ordered out and the defenceless aircraft was ruthlessly shot down.

Thirteen civilian passengers perished, and among them the well-known British film actor Leslie Howard, whose grace and gifts are still preserved for us by the records of the many delightful films in which he took part. The brutality of the Germans was only matched by the stupidity of their agents. It is difficult to understand how anyone in their senses could imagine that with all the resources of Great Britain at my disposal, I should have booked a passage in a neutral plane from Lisbon and flown home in broad daylight. We, of course, made a wide loop out by night from Gibraltar into the ocean and arrived home without incident. It was a painful shock to me to learn what had happened to others in the inscrutable workings of fate.[2]

That was the Churchill version, and the Germans were out to kill Churchill if they could. I myself heard of most secret German plans to assassinate him at the time of the Casablanca conference six months earlier. The order had come down from Hitler through Field Marshal Keitel to Admiral Canaris, Chief of Intelligence, and from him to the German Chief of Secret Operations, General Lahousen, who told me about it in 1950.[3] Sir Winston showed interest when I related this evidence and said, "Let me know if you glean any more information."

There was little more information to be gleaned on that score; for with the passing of the years, death and reticence stilled the loquacity of the Germans; but in 1951 a Dutch air pilot, Van Veenendaal, directed my attention again to the mystery of the airliner. Was this the real assassination attempt? He took an interest in it because it had been a Dutch plane and the pilot had been a friend of his. This incident, if clarified, might bring more revelations. Could the spy be found who reported that Churchill was on board? Who had given the order to shoot it down? Which pilot had fired the fateful burst?

The pathos of this story, the unexplained loss of Leslie Howard and his companions never ceased to interest me. He had meant so much to us all in his tireless and patriotic work during the war. His silent, wistful figure had vanished so suddenly and enigmatically. I determined to try and find the answer.

I looked for documents and eye-witnesses. There was hearsay and theory enough, and since it was not a technical failure, but an act of war, that had prevented this aircraft, G-AGBB, from reaching home, in order to find out the German motive it was essential to study the passenger list and know the crew as well. It was essential to find out what enemy aircraft had flown in that area at that time.

I investigated first the evidence that was already printed in communiques, in Hansard when Parliament debated the incident, and in various memoirs. As all that was inconclusive, I looked for more. In the course of travel, it seemed that coincidence brought me together with a number of people who were on the fringe of the mystery, who worked in Portugal during the war or flew in 1943 on the Lisbon route.[4] They offered their suggestions.

Who was the man who looked like Churchill and had, perhaps, paid for this likeness with his life? It was Alfred Chenhalls, a well-known international chartered accountant and Leslie Howard's income tax adviser.

He smoked big six-and-a-half-inch cigars like Churchill, was tubby and red-cheeked, and though younger and taller than the Prime Minister, might have been mistaken for him at a distance across the tarmac of an airport. He loved good clothes, bought his black Homburg hat in Bond Street, his suits and his blue Melton overcoat from the King's tailor, his cigars in St James's. He looked like a VIP.

He was a gay and sociable man, who knew most people of importance in the musical, literary, theatrical and film circles in London. His mission abroad in wartime? That does not seem to be clear. Officially he was accompanying Leslie Howard, who was on a lecture tour in Spain and Portugal, sponsored by the British Council.

Since the war we have learned that the British Secret Service placed a 'double' of Field Marshal Montgomery in Gibraltar to mislead the Germans at the time 'Monty' was about to launch the invasion of Normandy. But the appearance of Chenhalls in Portugal was quite a different thing. He had been there long enough for

Axis agents to know who he really was, and it was unthinkable that the British would place a decoy on board a civil airliner, even to ensure the safety of Mr Churchill's homeward flight.

Nevertheless spies can be very stupid in what they report, and if a false report was believed, that would account for the Lisbon incident.

Was it so fantastic to think that Churchill might have gone home via Portugal and flown in a civil aircraft? He was a man of surprise, risk stimulated him, his own staff were never sure what he would want to do next, and he had already once flown by civil airline in wartime across the Atlantic. That was in 1942, when he came home from Bermuda in the flying-boat *Berwick*, and moreover let a statement be issued on arrival to say that he had "been brought safely home by the British merchant air service".

Three years after the tragedy, Mrs Churchill met Alfred Chenhalls' widow at a dinner.

"It was dreadful how you lost your husband," said Mrs Churchill.

"If one of our husbands had to go, England could best spare mine," replied Mrs Chenhalls.

She added: "Perhaps if Alfred had not been so fond of cigars both he and Leslie Howard would have been alive today. But there is one consolation about Alfred's death. If he could have thought he was aiding Mr Churchill's safe return by misleading the enemy, I don't think he would have minded how he died."

* * *

This version of the story was believed by many people, but it was not entirely accepted by those who knew Leslie Howard. There were strong reasons to suggest that the film star himself had been a particular target of the Germans that day. If it was decided to interrupt the Lisbon-to-England air service, why not choose a day when some important person was travelling?

So reasoned Arthur Howard, his brother, and Ronald Howard,[5] actor son of the film star.

Leslie Howard was ostensibly on a lecture tour, but he may have been on some other more secret mission. He spoke fluent French and German; he had many friends in Austria before the war.

It was clear that the Germans showed a special interest in the movements of Leslie Howard. They detailed one of their agents to watch him in Madrid: a beautiful woman of Latin-American extraction. They planted another in his hotel in Estoril, and it has been confirmed to me by George West of the British Council that he was careful to warn Howard and Chenhalls of her presence.

Furthermore, there is the extraordinary story that Leslie Howard sent a letter from Lisbon to Madrid shortly before he took the plane for England, a letter addressed to the very woman who had been spying on him in Spain.

It was carried for him by Mr Neville Kearney, an official of the British Council, proceeding from Lisbon to Madrid on duty. Perhaps neither Leslie Howard nor Mr Kearney knew at first that they were in contact with an Axis spy: but in fact Howard was under close enemy observation from the very day he landed in Lisbon in April 1943 and began the lecture tour.

Dr Goebbels was known to detest him for his effective propaganda work and his scathing attacks on the Nazi way of life. Lord Haw-Haw[6] had threatened in his broadcasts to England to 'get' Howard when the Germans landed.

There has been a further story printed – the report that Howard had been friendly before the war with a woman film star of international repute, and so incurred the jealousy of Goebbels. So insatiable was the search for a motive that even that was examined.

Finally there is the evidence of Arthur Howard, himself in the

RAF, who took a keen interest after the war in what the Air Force interrogators had found out about his brother's death.

"The death of Leslie has never ceased to be a mystery to us," he told me. "We could not have known if he was on secret work abroad. I met some of our officers who interrogated German pilots, and they could recollect the incident of June 1st, 1943.

"These German pilots said that day after day they had spotted our airliners on the Lisbon route over the Bay of Biscay and reported them to base. But on this occasion when they reported it, the instruction came back – 'Shoot it down!'."

* * *

So there we have the conflicting theories. In one version a tall and well-built figure ambles towards the tarmac smoking a cigar; in the other there is a woman international spy, watching someone who is (with the Germans) a most unpopular man.

Chapter 2

The Search

Some bits of the puzzle have fitted, and others cannot be forced together. The neat and finished artistry of fiction brings in its characters at the right moments and asks them to play well-defined dramatic parts; but this search is, as Leslie Howard would have said: "full of unexplainable loose ends". Many people met on the Lisbon scene in wartime and reappear briefly in this investigation. They cannot be discarded, because they may have some essential fact to divulge. Every passenger has to be 'screened', for in wartime people often travel under false names, and there may have been a third man on board whose role was just as significant as that of Leslie Howard or the man who looked like Churchill.

Some facts can be found to support every theory but not all of them can be reconciled to one theory. The first report of the tragedy is short and enigmatic. You can find it in the cuttings of any newspaper library, for it was a story that went round the world. This is how it was reported on 3 June 1943 :

'We are being attacked by enemy aircraft.'

That message was sent out from a British Overseas airliner over the Bay of Biscay on its way home from Lisbon. After that, there was silence.

Last night came the news that the plane carrying thirteen passengers including Leslie Howard, the stage and screen actor, and a crew of four, had been shot down by the Luftwaffe.

British Overseas Airways Corporation say that the plane must be presumed lost. It was on its way from Lisbon to a British airport.

The aircraft, a DC-3 liner, left Lisbon on Tuesday morning at 9.30. The last communication received from it was at 11 o'clock. It was then being attacked over the Bay of Biscay.

Yesterday a German communique said: 'German reconnaissance planes shot down three enemy bombers and one transport over the Atlantic' The transport was undoubtedly Leslie Howard's.'

Parliamentary questions brought no enlightenment.

On 9 June Sir Archibald Sinclair, the Air Minister, rose to tell the House of Commons that steps had been taken to reduce the risks that airliners must face on the Lisbon-England route.

He was asked by Sir Malcolm Robertson (Conservative, Mitcham) whether instructions would be given that the practice of airliners leaving Lisbon by daylight must cease, in view of the danger involved owing to the presence at Lisbon of enemy agents. Sir Malcolm, as Chairman of the British Council, was responsible for the tour of Leslie Howard, and must have received special reports on the incident from his staff in Lisbon.[1] His question implied that enemy agents had been active, either in reporting the time of departure of the plane or something of importance about it.

Sir Archibald replied that no trace of the aircraft or its occupants had been found. He said that the risks of interception, and the routes and schedules to be followed, had been kept under review since the service had started three years previously. He declared:

"That only one incident has occurred since then shows that no undue risks have been taken. With the increase of intensity in air warfare over the Bay of Biscay, certain further steps have been taken to reduce the chances of interception. It would not be in the public interest to give them."

Nothing more was said at the time and apart from Sir Winston

Churchill's own version, nothing authoritative has been added since.

Such was the story as once more I propounded it to an old American friend of the Central Intelligence Agency as we sat over dinner at the Carriage House outside Washington years afterwards:

"Ah, so you're on to that story," said the American. "There was something curious about that aircraft."

"What do you mean? Is it true that the Germans believed Churchill was on board?" I asked him. "Or was it an act of revenge against Leslie Howard?"

"I don't know the truth about that," he said, shaking his head. "There was just something about that aircraft, but it's not my secret. I heard something in the course of duty. I can't repeat it. I'm sure I don't even know the whole story."

He beamed at me in a most friendly manner. I had known him for many years as a serious witness, once the correspondent in Europe of an American newspaper and later one of Allen Dulles' young men in the Central Intelligence Agency. Allen, the brother of John Foster Dulles, had worked in Switzerland during the war on most secret contacts with opponents of Hitler inside Germany.

"Surely there can be no harm in telling me now, ten years after. Was there a secret American courier on board that plane, or vital intelligence material?"

He shook his head and smiled.

"Was there an important refugee from Germany? Was one of the passengers under an assumed name?"

He beamed again and said no more, except:

"It would make a great difference to your story to know, but I'm not the man to tell you, and I don't suppose you'll ever guess it."

I was bound to respect his desire not to impart a secret of the intelligence service even years after the event. But others might be able to tell me more.

"Go to the top every time, if there's something you want," said a wise old friend of mine. So I asked to see Allen Dulles himself.

Now, Allen Dulles is the ears and eyes of the US Government. As head of the Central Intelligence Agency, he would know what the mystery of that aircraft was, if it had in any way concerned the wartime office of Strategic Services in which he worked. I went to Dulles' office and asked him point blank.

A genial head, kindly eyes, and that trick effect in important men of seeming slightly larger than human size – such was my impression of Dulles. He listened attentively to my theory about the aircraft that was shot down.

"Perhaps there was an important courier on board," I suggested, "with information that it was vital for the Germans to intercept – an emissary perhaps coming to offer peace behind the back of Hitler, or another Rudolf Hess case."

Dulles thought back and said:

"No, I don't see that we were at all concerned in the case of that aircraft. You see, I did not send my information from Switzerland by courier. We used cipher radio messages at that time."

He could throw no light on the mystery. I thanked him and left him there at his desk in Washington, engaged in a much harder task than ever confronted him in his secret war against the Germans in 1943. All that remained to me was to re-examine such evidence as existed, scrutinise the passenger list, and see what living witnesses could be found.

The strange thing to me was that the enigma should have been allowed to remain so long unsolved. There might be a reason for that, too, some point of secrecy that could still not be cleared for the public.

* * *

This was apparently the only fatal incident in three years of flying the Lisbon route. I found several witnesses to support the general theory that the German Secret Service did not wish these airliners to be attacked.

General Erwin Lahousen, the German wartime head of sabotage, wrote to tell me that his Chief, Admiral Canaris, expressly forbade him to organise sabotage operations against civil aircraft from neutral territory. Lahousen covered himself by recording this ruling in the war diary of his branch. Canaris went specially to Lisbon to warn his intelligence officers not to allow acts of violence involving loss of civilian life to be organised in Portugal.[2]

Could the aircraft have been intercepted on any flight? To that question Allied Intelligence men who sat in Lisbon gave me a clear answer. It was impossible to keep the time of departure of the British airliner secret. It flew by daylight to a fairly regular schedule. The passengers had to walk past the office of the German Lufthansa to reach the tarmac. The Germans in 1936 had helped to install a navigational beacon along the northern coast of Spain. In 1940 they extended it along the Biscay coast of France. However, this beacon system could not have helped to intercept the airliner as radar might have done. Weighing these arguments, I see this list of possibilities:

1. The aircraft was shot down because it was believed that Churchill was on board – Churchill had said so.
2. The aircraft was shot down because of Nazi animosity towards Leslie Howard – the Howard family believed this.
3. The aircraft was shot down because it was vital to the Germans that some third person should not reach England – a new theory.
4. The pilot or the crew may have been working against the Germans – this version was current in Lisbon too.
5. The aircraft was shot down in a chance encounter – but why had that not happened before?

6. The aircraft was mistaken for a military machine – but it plainly had civil markings.

And what of the passenger list? What clues could that give us? I have been over the passenger list, and asked questions of the Departments that sponsored travel, and the friends and relatives who knew why these people were travelling. A certificate from the Portuguese Customs[3] shows that there were thirteen passengers that day:

Mr Alfred Tregear Chenhalls,
Mr Francis German Cowlrick,
Mr Leslie Howard,
Mrs Rotha Violet Lettie Hutcheon,
    Carola Hutcheon,
    Petra Hutcheon,
Mr Wilfrid Jacob Berthold Israel,
Mr Gordon Thompson Maclean,
Mrs Cecilia Amelia Falla Paton,
Mr Ivan James Sharp,
Mr Tyrrell Milmay Shervington,
Mr Kenneth Stonehouse,
Mrs Evelyn Stonehouse.

We know about Alfred Chenhalls, the finance expert with the offices in Chancery Lane, who managed the financial side of Leslie Howard Productions Ltd – the man with the cigar, who went to make a films promotion tour of Spain and Portugal.[4]

Francis Cowlrick was an elderly engineer working for a British firm who had long been resident in Spain. He was returning home on retirement – so I was told in Madrid.

Leslie Howard, the man who angered Goebbels with his films of Nazi types and the deathless story of the Battle of Britain Spitfire,

'The First of the Few', the man who wore himself out in the war years, and was still hard at work when he boarded the plane in Lisbon.

Wilfrid Jacob Berthold Israel – an interesting passenger, this. He was working for the Jewish Agency in Spain and Portugal, trying to get young Jewish volunteers out of the clutches of Hitler.

Gordon Thompson Maclean, an elderly Foreign Office man, was on a tour of inspection of British embassies and consulates abroad. The Foreign Office tells me that he was on no special mission. He was making a survey of the expenses of the diplomatic service in that war era of rising prices.

Tyrrell Milmay Shervington, the manager in Lisbon of the Shell-Mex Corporation. He was returning to London for family reasons, to see his son, who was going on active service.[5]

Kenneth Stonehouse, the Washington correspondent of Reuters, was on his way to take up a war correspondent's job.

Ivan James Sharp, a mining engineer and an official of the United Kingdom Commercial Corporation, had been on a tour of Spanish and Portuguese mines to report on wolfram, a product vital to the war effort of Britain and her allies, vital also to the Axis Powers.

Such was the business of the passengers. There may be another story to each one of them, and we shall see what else there is to tell of the movements and identity of these thirteen. I have been going through contemporary files of Portuguese papers, examining letters and official records, questioning friends and the civil airline officials of four nations. I have checked with the former British air attaché, Wing Commander Schreiber, and the Portuguese Customs. None of these men was travelling incognito. There was apparently nobody else on board who was not shown on the passenger list.

And the women? Mrs Rotha Violet Hutcheon, British born, and

her daughters Carola and Petra, were on their way back from America to join Lieutenant Colonel Hutcheon RA, who was with the Canadian forces in the United Kingdom.

Mrs Cecilia Falla Paton was going to take up a secretarial job at the Cuban consulate in Liverpool. She was put on the aircraft at short notice when another passenger was taken off.[6]

Mrs Evelyn Stonehouse was accompanying her husband home to Britain. She too wanted to do war work. She had seen enough of the pleasant life of Washington.

The crew? These were Quirinus Tepas OBE, an old and tried pilot of the Royal Dutch Airlines, his second officer, Captain D. de Koning, his wireless operator, Cornelis van Brugge, and his flight engineer, Engbertus Rosevink. The records of these men, as shown to me by the Royal Dutch Airlines, are simply those of a highly-trained air crew. They had also been under the close watch of the British Secret Service, both in England and in Portugal, long enough for it to be beyond doubt that they were ordinary flying personnel.

The passenger list by itself does not give us the answer, and a second check on the movements and activities of the passengers seems to indicate nothing that was not already known.

I turned to the Service Ministries in Whitehall, to see if they had a solution. The Air Ministry and the Ministry of Defence have given a good deal of thought and study to the case, but apparently found no fresh evidence or complete explanations. At British Overseas Airways there were no documents relating to it. They thought there might be something to be learned from Royal Dutch Airlines, from whom the aircraft was on wartime charter.

"Ah, yes," said the Dutch airline officials. "There was a small group of Dutch civil aircraft under Captain Parmentier that flew in wartime on the Lisbon line, but if there are any papers in existence on this case, they will be in the Netherlands."

I flew to the Schiphol Airport at Amsterdam, which I had not visited since the war. There lay the runways and hangars among the polders and canals of the neat Dutch landscape. Beyond the airport buildings were hutments used as a registry, where some archives of the airline had been stored.

"Captain Parmentier was here after the war," said the keeper of the registry. "He left some papers with us then."

He walked up and down the bookcases and pointed to a row of box-files on a high shelf.

"Parmentier brought those back from England with him in 1944. Nobody has opened them since. Perhaps you will discover what you want there. Perhaps you will make a find."

I took down one file after the other and looked at their closely packed contents. These were the flight reports and administrative orders of the air crews who had kept open the London–Lisbon line during the years of Hitler's ascendency in Europe. Soon I came upon the name of Tepas, and that of his aircraft, PH-ALI in the Dutch markings, changed to G-AGBB when BOAC took over the Dutch aircraft. This was the one that vanished. It was named the *Ibis*. I brushed the dust of ten years off more files and found a lot of correspondence with the Civil Aviation branch of the Air Ministry. There were letters marked 'Secret' and 'Most Secret'. There were reports on all the movements of the aircraft itself.

It was like walking back a dozen years into the blackout, and seeing those few aircraft coming and going on the Lisbon line, and knowing the men who flew them under their own particular stresses. If the stories of the passengers could be added to theirs, the true picture might form. This inquiry had taken me from England to Holland. It leads to Lisbon and Madrid, and to Germany.

The *Ibis* was evidently singled out for a special fate. She was the first of the all-metal DC-3 aircraft to go into service in Europe. She was frequently mentioned in these Schiphol archives. Strange luck and strange misfortune pursued her after the British had daubed her gleaming skin with matt camouflage paint in 1940 and set her flying on the passenger route to Lisbon.

Day after day her Dutch crews took her to and fro, and on to Gibraltar, until finally up came something like a treble on a fruit machine – Flight 777. And on that flight she vanished without trace and without explanation. What the Germans would call a *spurlose Verschwindung.*

Having retraced her story that far, I feel I can attempt to relate what happened, and first of all how this Dutch aircraft came to be flying for Britain in wartime on the Lisbon line. Looking out of the windows of the Schiphol with these documents on the table, the scene reconstructs itself.

Chapter 3

The *Ibis*

"Quirinus, it will be your flight!"

Koene Dirk Parmentier, senior Dutch pilot, stood outside the Schiphol offices and watched them servicing the *Ibis*. It was 9 May 1940. Parmentier was a masterful man, short and powerfully built, abrupt and determined in his movements. His hard blue eyes, aquiline nose, straight thin lips, and square jaw were all expressive of energy and command. The upper lip seemed unusually extended and his mouth was drawn together in a decisive expression. He had been the pilot of the DC-2 airliner which won the handicap section of the London-Melbourne air race in 1934, just behind Campbell and Black in the de Havilland 88. And that gave him thereafter, or so some of the less eminent pilots fancied, the trace of a swagger.

But that swagger would still have been worn had Parmentier never taken part in the Melbourne race; for he was also outstanding as an administrator – half the battle in successful civil flying.

By contrast the pilot he spoke to, Quirinus Tepas, was a mild, serene-looking man. A snub nose, round blue eyes, and fair curly hair gave him a cherubic appearance. He and Parmentier had flown the *Ibis* many times on the Jakarta route since she first came to Europe from the Douglas assembly lines in 1936.

"Yes, my flight," Tepas replied and walked over to inspect the cockpit. For a moment he looked up at her and the mechanics clambering on her wing.

If *Ibis* had been built for beauty only, she could not have had neater lines. The surging lines of throat and belly streamed cleanly with leading edge and tail. She was powered by two Wright Cyclone

1,000–horse-power engines. Her wing-span was ninety-five feet, her length sixty-four; her highest speed was 210 mph; her cruising speed 165 mph; she could fly to a maximum height of 23,000 feet, but having regard to her payload and the fact that she was unpressurised, 12,000 feet was about her service limit. She carried a crew of four – a pilot, co–pilot, wireless operator, and flight engineer – and twenty-one passengers.[1] Her name was painted to port and starboard of her nose in small square lettering, orange on silver.

The *Ibis* was a luxury airliner. The Dakota or C-47, a utility version of the same aircraft, had not yet left the assembly lines to earn the title 'workhorse of the air' over the battle areas of the Second World War.

The *Ibis* had sister aircraft: *Heron, Buzzard, Aigrette, Curlew,* and others in the bird class. They were flying to European capitals from Schiphol. For two years *Ibis* had flown the Jakarta route to the Dutch East Indies. Her papers showed me that early in 1939 she was recalled and put on the European network, and that on 9 May 1940 she was standing by to take the next flight from Amsterdam to Shoreham.

Today the DC-3 is outstripped and left behind by newer and faster types. In *Jane's Aircraft,* the social register of the air, I find her referred to in the 'Who Was Who' of flying. She figures in the index only. Her picture graces the illustrations of *Jane's* no more; there are monsters with four and six engines to impress you instead. Their range, ceiling, and speed make *Ibis* seem slow and old-fashioned; but some machines of the DC-3 design are still flying today, twenty years after the first came to Europe.

It was with the *Ibis* papers like turning over the album of a well-remembered star, who keeps our affection long after younger performers have supplanted her. She still has it for looks over many more modern planes. She was a beautiful aircraft.

The Schiphol records showed only slight alterations of schedule at the beginning of the war. Croydon ceased to be the port of call in England. The Dutch aircraft were switched to Shoreham in Kent for security reasons. They received instructions about the strict limits of Channel flying and the danger to aircraft passing over ships of the Royal Navy. New officials arrived at Shoreham and organised new procedure for clearing passengers. The word 'Security' was printed large and posters at the airport showed the grim effects of careless talk.

So there were long delays recorded in the early days of the war in moving aircraft and passengers. Sometimes a scheduled flight would be cancelled for no apparent reason, with no fog at either airport. Sometimes the impatient passengers stamped and muttered that something bad must have happened in the Netherlands.

Yet when the delays of September 1939 were over *Ibis* flew regularly for seven months between Shoreham and the familiar parking hangars at the Schiphol, A, B, and C; and the workshop hangar. But for the gunsites on the airport, the Dutch scene was peaceful and unaltered.

England itself was quiet, though civilians carried gasmask haversacks to the office and stuck strips of tape across their windows. The air war had not really begun.

The Americans studied the lull in Europe, and called it a 'phoney war', until in April 1940 Denmark and Norway were invaded and overrun. There was nothing phoney about that. And this was 9 May.

All was still quiet in the West, but that day there was anxiety in the Netherlands. A whole series of precautionary measures had been taken at the frontiers, and the Dutch forces were at a state of alert. No evacuation of aircraft had taken place. The Dutch civil air fleet stood ready for their scheduled flights, but there was an unusual feature about the Schiphol tarmac on 9 May. None of the ugly Junkers 52 with their red–white–black Swastika markings landed or took off. Civil flying was suspended between Germany and the Netherlands.

Ibis was scheduled to leave as usual next morning for Shoreham, and when Parmentier had seen her serviced he walked thoughtfully back to the airline offices and later than usual left for home.

There was much uneasiness, he thought, but there had been alarms before in November 1939 and January 1940. Each time the tense calm had not been broken – it had been a false alarm or Hitler had ordered postponement.

But as Parmentier was sitting down to dinner in his villa near the airport, the Dutch intelligence service in Berlin was probing what the morrow held in store, and this time there was no doubt about it at all.

That evening a German contact man of the Dutch military attaché in Berlin slipped into the German High Command and ascertained what was afoot. The attack on the West was to start before daybreak.

"It's the end now," he whispered to the waiting Dutch attaché as he came out. "The top swine has left for the front. There has been no countermand."

From the Legation at 10.20 pm the Dutch military attaché put through a call and spoke to the Duty Officer in Headquarters at The Hague on the open telephone.

"Lieutenant, you know my voice," he said. "I have only one thing to tell you. Tomorrow at dawn. Hold tight! You understand me?"

"Is this message 210?"

"Yes, it is message 210. Goodnight."

In The Hague it was a clear spring evening. The Dutch Foreign Minister, Dr Van Kleffens, had gone out for a short walk with his wife, to get some fresh air after a heavy day at the office. At 9.30 he had just come in.

"I received a telephone message from the War Office: serious news. There had been a warning of a German attack on the Low

Countries, given by our Intelligence Service: it contained just five words. 'Tomorrow at dawn. Hold tight!'

"From a military point of view there was little more that could be done," he said. Flooding would not take place before an invasion actually started.

The Dutch Cabinet Ministers sat up late that night, smoking cigars and waiting. Just before 4 am the telephone rang. It was to inform them that Schiphol, Waalhaven, Bergen, and de Kooy airfields had been bombed.

"Daylight fell almost surprisingly, at this hour of four o'clock, upon us. I had a feeling of numb coldness. Then suddenly Hell burst loose around us as the anti-aircraft guns came into action against ever-increasing swarms of German planes, bombing barracks on the outskirts of the town."

Back to Schiphol, where Dutch fighter aircraft were taking off as the bombs fell, hurried Dirk Parmentier. He met hurrying air crews and mechanics on the way. They knew that the precious airliners were still in the hangars. In the five hours since the warning from Berlin, no evacuation order had reached Schiphol. It was still dark, and overhead in the darkness droned heavy engines with an ominous sound.

"At about 3 am," said Parmentier, "a large number of unidentified aircraft flew at a high altitude in a westerly direction over Schiphol and disappeared in the direction of the North Sea. All military aircraft were parked outside the actual airport, but were taxied back and made serviceable."

At exactly 4 am the first German bombers came in from the direction of the sea, whence they were least expected. A flash and a roar of bombs showed a direct hit on the military barracks in the east corner of the airport. Other squadrons arrived from all sides and a shower of incendiaries fell on hangars and buildings. All Dutch fighter aircraft took off. Some of them were actually taking off during the bombing. They were attacked by twin-engined Messerschmitts, which also turned their machine guns on the anti-aircraft posts, soldiers, and aircraft dispersed over the airport.

The Dutch gunners fired back hard, traversing and blazing away at each attack. The planes were coming in waves of two or three squadrons at intervals of fifteen to twenty minutes.

"There go our fighters after him."

A Dornier flying with one dead engine went slowly overhead, losing height, towards Amsterdam.

Parmentier watched it fly right over his house and disappear behind trees.

Over came another flight of five bombers in V formation.

"They're at about 500 feet now, and they're going for the anti-aircraft guns along the Spaarnhouderweg."

Between raids the Dutch pilots and ground staff drove, bicycled, and ran through Amsterdam to reach the airport and try to save their aircraft.

Six armoured cars guarded the Schiphol against glider landings and paratroops. Four anti-aircraft guns and two anti-aircraft cannon were emplaced against low-flying aircraft. One of these machine-gun posts had received a direct hit, but the others were intact and blazed away at the lean, fleeting forms with the black crosses on their wings.

Air reconnaissance must have showed the Germans that it was foolish to try and land there. Blocks of concrete and parked buses denied them those Schiphol runways which were not guarded by the gun-posts.

The first target for rescue was the barracks. About fifty troops and Amsterdam firemen had been killed and a large number wounded. The Bovenheck guns helped to keep reconnoitring German aircraft at a distance, and the Germans did not come back in force after their first raid. They had easier targets elsewhere. Schiphol was a tough proposition to capture. Besides, the first raid had done effective damage. The military barracks had burned out completely. The neat little Dutch houses on the Ringvaart Canal and Plesman Lane were roofless, windowless, and some were blown to bits or burnt out. The airport canteen was blazing, though the military hangars east of the runways had no more damage than broken skylights.

"Help us to clear Hangar A," shouted Parmentier.

He led in the airport staff, looking round warily for signs of unexploded bombs. They dragged out of Hangar A one undamaged airliner and some motor buses. They put out a fire between two of the hangars and found Hangar B with an airliner burnt out and the wreckage of others strewn all around it. The instrument shop was intact. In Hangar C were more casualties.

Parmentier in his shirtsleeves hurried on to the central workshop in Hangar D. This was a graveyard of aircraft. The spare-parts store was badly damaged by fire, the blackened skeletons of three Douglas aircraft and a training machine sprawled in the wreckage; two more DC-3s were badly damaged by fire. Direct hits had riddled and burst open several others; the boiler-house had a direct hit. The choking smell of destruction was all around them. They could not even disperse the undamaged aircraft, as the blast of high explosives had buckled and jammed the hangar doors. But the runway itself was little damaged, so the planes parked about the airport had suffered less.

And what of the *Ibis* that day? She was standing outside on the tarmac. Parmentier walked round her, inspecting the damage. Bomb-splinters had torn fuselage, wings, and controls; and the tail surfaces were seriously ripped.

"She can be made serviceable," he said. "There are three other DC-3s repairable. Volunteers for repair work!"

The ground staff toiled for three days on the damaged aircraft. They counted neither time nor overtime. On 13 May there were ten airliners nearly airworthy. Two serviceable machines were held at the disposal of General Winkelmann, the Commander-in-Chief. Eight had been written off.

But on 13 May the Germans crossed the Ijssel and Maas in force, outflanking the Dutch fortified line. They had reached the Meuse in the Ardennes and captured Liège. It was plain that the British and French armies could not reach Holland by land. There were no reserves to send by sea. The Dutch Government took the grave decision to move to Great Britain.

On the day of that decision, Mr Churchill, his war Cabinet just two days old, uttered the words that were at once an inspiration to the British and a warning to those who would share our lot.

"I have nothing to offer but blood and toil and tears and sweat."

These words pierced the confusion of war and the confusion of tongues. The Dutch mechanics, with spanners poised over the battered aircraft, heard them and pondered as they worked on. They were heard and repeated on that day throughout the Netherlands. Parmentier and his fellow pilots made their choice – but it was not so easy to get to England.

Ibis, after emergency repairs, could just fly, though her port engine was faulty. She was not fully airworthy, so the Dutch armed forces had not commandeered her for transport duties.

At 5 pm on 13 May Parmentier ceased to shake his head at her port engine. He realised that it was now or never, and there were crews who would fly with him in an unserviceable aircraft rather than wait till the Germans marched in. With a scratch crew he hurried on board, swung her on to the runway, and, risking being shot down at any moment, headed the limping bird for the North

Sea and Shoreham. A day later German air superiority was such that *Ibis* could not have left the ground.

On the 14th a mass raid gutted the centre of Rotterdam, killing 30,000 burghers in the cold plan to compel the stubborn Dutch to give up the fight, and so after five days' fighting the Germans achieved what they had expected to accomplish in one.

"If we had not capitulated then," another pilot, Theo Verhoeven, told me, "they would have destroyed Leyden, Amsterdam, and The Hague in the same manner as Rotterdam until they forced the Netherlands army to lay down its arms."

Verhoeven was stationed in May 1940 as a military flying instructor on an island in the North Sea named Schouwenpluivenland – the land of doves. He too slipped out of Holland via Breskens, hitch-hiked with the stream of refugees through France to Berck-sur-Mer, Abbeville, Dieppe, Caen. He embarked at Cherbourg and landed in Milford Haven at the same time as the British Expeditionary Force and First French Army were crowding into the little ships off Dunkirk to be ferried home.

The decision had been previously taken that in the event of invasion the Dutch airline would transfer its head offices to the East Indies, and re-organise its world services from there, except for those planes which could be got to England to be put at the disposal of the Netherlands Government in exile. This was how Dutch aircraft and crews became available to fly from Britain on the wartime route to Lisbon.

Parmentier landed the *Ibis* at Shoreham. The British mechanics with simple professional interest walked round her and inspected the hastily patched damage, and listened to her port engine. Soon they would take her to Ringway, Manchester, for repairs, daub over the sheen of her sides with drab camouflage paint,[2] cover up the

Dutch number and the name *Ibis,* and give her a British identification number instead.

I have heard that the only thing left to show what she had once been was a trick in her camouflage pattern. They painted on to her fuselage the outline of the lost provinces of the Netherlands. I have not been able to confirm the point, but it is nice to think that it was so.

Meanwhile, by the slow processes of war routine, the characters who would fly in the *Ibis* were brought together in space and time.

Chapter 4

Enter Leslie Howard

It is one day early in August 1939 that Leslie Howard makes his entry. You could not fix that for certain, for there was something too inconsequent and vague about his movements. Introspective and uncommunicative, in the same way he strayed on and off the set, always in doubt, it seemed, whether he was a spectator, a director, or a mere actor. But when he suddenly remembered, or was suddenly reminded, that this was his entry and there were his lines, he quietly folded his spectacles and slipped away; and when, a second or so later, he re-emerged on the set, there was no longer any doubt about what he was.

I see him in this first scene sitting rather low in an easy-chair in his library in the white house on Beverly Hills, browsing over a book, propping his pipe with the other hand, and hoping that the telephone would not ring.

Of course it did, and the voice had a strong American business intonation.

"Leslie, what's this I hear that you may be going off to Britain?"

"Maybe is right. I'm thinking about it."

"You're not forgetting that you're signed up with us for a film?"

"I'm not forgetting that you want me to make a film. In fact I am very seriously considering that very point."

"What do you mean, Leslie?"

"Well, I think that as you read the newspapers and listen to the radio, you must see there's a war coming in Europe, and I am thinking of my own country. If America were attacked, where would you be?"

"Right here," said the American voice, "till I was called up."

"Well, in a sense I feel I am being called up already."

"Nobody's calling you up, Leslie. There are some things you can't do to United Players, and one is to walk out on 'Bonnie Prince Charlie'."

"Well, I'm the only person who can decide that."

"You're a crazy guy, Leslie. I'll be round to see you in the morning. And you'll change your mind. And you'll stay here."

Leslie would put down the telephone and put down the book too, and look into space. Well, at forty-six he had had a wonderful career. It had taken him from the prospects of a £2 10s.-a-week bank clerk into the £1,000-a-week class. Moreover it had placed him so that he could, and perhaps would, turn down Hollywood's £40,000 a year, and not miss it.

What had built up this slight, fair-haired young English actor – he still looked in the middle thirties – to command such astonishing prices? Part of the answer came from the playwright A. E. Thomas when he wrote in the *Saturday Evening Post* in the late 'twenties:

> There are not in the whole of the United States more than a dozen young American actors competent to play leading parts in a comedy of manners, charm and breeding. The English on the contrary breed these actors in considerable numbers.

And high up in that talent scale was Leslie Howard. To his early gift for dramatics, developed young in amateur theatricals at Dulwich College, Leslie brought a studious mind. A "very dreamy and vague little boy", he had written short stories and plays, wanting above all to be a writer. His businessman father had wished him to go into a bank, but the First World War brought an end to parental influence over many young men, and after it Leslie set out instead on a tour of

England with a theatrical company. Yet it was a serious venture. Before he went he sat for three weeks in the stalls of a London theatre studying the part he was to play. He was learning, and learning hard.

"I admit I'm confoundedly independent. I never take a part if I feel it's unsuited to me."

He said that years later, but when he arrived on Broadway in the early twenties he took whatever part he could get. It was mostly in English plays, and very English parts they were.

Quite a number of those plays had been flops, so the New York critics got used to writing quite often a nice word about the young English actor, though they killed stone dead the play in which he was acting. It was a precarious, exciting, and exacting life for a young man starting family life.

Ruth Howard managed him, worked over his parts with him, kept him properly dressed. Nobody, in assessing the early success story, can overlook the wife of Leslie Howard. A firm and robust nature, energetic and ambitious for him, she compensated for the unfailing modesty of her husband, convincing them all that even in a small part he was showing how much more he could do.

"I tell you, he's a wonderful actor," she would exclaim, bustling about behind the set and impressing everybody she met.

They had to take what parts Leslie could get. Yet the independent spirit was already there. He was not going to have his own taste overridden. Those parts he could act, he wanted to play as he saw them. That was why he was in doubt about 'Her Cardboard Lover'.

It is wrongly supposed that it was Tallulah Bankhead who made his name for him in that play. It happened quite differently. The first lady to play the leading part with Leslie Howard supporting was an American actress called Jeanne Eagels,[1] compared with whom Miss Bankhead was a homely and sensible girl.

Jeanne Eagels, while her name shone large in the lights of Broadway, was everything that Leslie detested in an actress. She doped, she drank, she was domineering and passionate. She was unpunctual and at times her show on Broadway had to close down, because she simply disappeared from ken for days at a time.

All this had made rehearsing with Jeanne a torment for the young English actor. He had his own part worked out, but she would not let him play it that way.

"Leslie darling, you mustn't do that at this moment," she drawled. "I'm going to be doing this, and it takes attention off what I am doing."

Twice he walked out of rehearsals, and once he decided to throw it up altogether. Yet he went on. But after a towering row, Leslie seemed to give way and rehearsed just as she wanted him to – enough and no more. It was as if she had in fact reduced him to papier mâché.

When the first night came, as soon as the curtain was up Leslie discarded his rehearsed part altogether. Everything that he had wished to put into the play, he did. The effect was amazing. Not only had he the audience watching him, but he had Jeanne Eagels watching him too and wondering what he would do next. He did not take the final curtain, but went straight to his dressing-room, where he could still hear the roar of the audience. And then above it the insistent knocking of Jeanne Eagels on his door – and that familiar drawl:

"Leslie, darling, it's *you* they're calling for."

That was a great day.

A delighted critic, Alexander Woollcott, wrote of this performance in the *Sunday World* of 22 March 1922:

I do not wish to suggest that it was the gala audience who boorishly intruded on Miss Eagel's ovations by yelling for her leading man. The whole audience's response to his airy and adroit performance was audibly unanimous, but the mischievous shouting for him by name may have come from a mere handful. Why, if only those actors who had been ousted from the cast during rehearsals, because Miss Eagels did not approve of them, had managed to get seats, they could have worked the entire demonstration unaided.

But one success of that kind could not have made his reputation unless there was much more to him, and unless Fortune was going to go on knocking on his dressing-room door.

She knocked consistently with offers of good parts, because here was the apotheosis of the restrained modern male. Leslie Howard was developing a new form of contact with his audience, away from the obvious rant and swagger of the stage. One critic described it as "always saying something before he speaks", and another "all understanding and sensitivity, and with it a faintly casual air as if his charm was nothing out of the ordinary". It was that, of course, that sent the tingles down the spines of the Hollywood women gossip-writers.

He toured England with Tallulah Bankhead[2] in 'Her Cardboard Lover', and then returned to America and yielded at last in 1930 to the call of Hollywood. He was to make the film of 'Outward Bound', the play about a number of passengers who find themselves on board a liner without being quite certain what their destination is. After a while it becomes clear to them that they are dead and that the liner is taking them on to the next world.

More than one of his early parts had this symbol of the supernatural in it. He played Peter Standish in 'Berkeley Square', the man who goes back a century in time and falls in love with a beauty of Regency London. Strange parts, strangely well played.

Heather Angel acted opposite him in the film version of 'Berkeley Square'. Her mother, watching him in the love scenes, noticed this strange quality – "he has that marvellous power on the screen of showing his thoughts without moving a muscle of his face. It's some power that comes from within." A power not easy to define.

That was perhaps why Howard, when he was not wandering off to direct the show, always went for the quiet parts, the mysticism of 'Outward Bound' appealed to him, and some thought 'Berkeley Square' his first big stage success. That too was a great day.

As Sir Percy Blakeney in 'The Scarlet Pimpernel', Leslie exploited that nonchalant, deceptive appearance that was part of his nature and made another hit that is still remembered.

Hollywood had to pull hard to get him away from Broadway, even for a part in 'Outward Bound'. The calm and maddening resistance which he showed to the frantic pace of Hollywood put his price even higher. Plainly he could not be bought for a part.

There was the time that Marion Davies offered him £16,000 to play opposite her in 'Peg O' My Heart', and offered Ruth Howard a commission to persuade him to agree to do so.

"If you can persuade him to do it," said Marion, "you can go to Cartier's and buy any diamond bracelet up to five thousand dollars as your commission."

Leslie had not needed the part, and, what is much more, he had not wanted it, so he turned it down. A great day, too, when he could afford to do that.

Then he was offered the role opposite Greta Garbo in her film 'Queen Christina', and he had turned down that as well. What the Snow Queen said is not recorded.

It was not so much out of disdain for Hollywood, as for something he didn't like about a part. For he accepted Hollywood as Hollywood learned to accept him, and sometimes he felt uncertain as to where he rightly belonged in the world. He had a strangely humble and enduring love for England, and yet America exerted an overpowering fascination on him.

The British critics saw him slowly becoming an American – "like all Englishmen who stay long in America, he had that subtle half-American look that comes from wearing American shirts and shoes."

In the middle 1930s he thought he had solved this dual allegiance by buying a house in Surrey – Stowe Maries at Westcott. It was an ample but not luxurious English country house of nine bedrooms. A great acquisition to make after only fifteen years at his trade.

But the critics, who note everything, said in 1933 that he looked like a man who has achieved the dream of a lifetime and is not quite sure that he wants it all. The urge for America was returning.

He was back there in 1935, vexed by dual tax problems, and seriously thinking of taking out American papers when, with a splendour of scarlet and gold and horsehair plumes, the Jubilee celebrations of King George V drew the eyes of the world to London. Leslie, overcome with being English, went to the microphone and in a broadcast to America said very simply that the Jubilee had brought home to him "the knowledge of all that a democratic monarchy means". He could not now take up American nationality. The broadcast was a tremendous hit. That too had been a great day.

The man who sat dreamily in the library at Beverly Hills in 1939 must have thought back to other moments.

The day in 1936 when he returned to Westcott with a string of polo ponies and a Texan rancher to manage them. There were once as many as sixteen ponies. Hunting and hacking round the Surrey lanes with his children, Ronald and Ruth Leslie, polo at Ranelagh, parties at the Savoy. And then once more the tug of America, and the impulsive desire to put across his ideas on Hamlet in New York.

Putting on 'Hamlet' in Boston and Broadway, and refusing Orson Welles the chance to do murder in the part of King Claudius. Himself a pale and rather quiet Hamlet – too quiet for some of the critics. Refusing a contract for £150,000, because it would have tied him to accept parts he didn't like. "I want to direct more and act less. I must have a free hand," he pleaded.

Hiding from thousands of fans at the stage door, collar up, hat over face, dark glasses. Hiding from the public, who hailed him as "the great lover" of the screen – "a terribly low standard of appreciation," he remarked wryly. Hiding because he genuinely detested the fuss.

He paced about the library, hands stuck deep in the pockets of his grey slacks. August 1939: what to do now? His whole life had been one of uncertain movements, and it was uncanny that despite this apparent vagueness, he had not yet put a foot wrong.

The filming of 'Pygmalion' was behind him, the filming of 'Gone with the Wind' had been finished that spring, with Leslie in the lesser role of Ashley Wilkes. He had finished 'Intermezzo' and he wanted an increasing hand in direction.

Leslie Howard in August 1939 to be making a film of 'Bonnie Prince Charlie'? Nuts!

He had other ideas, and he walked outside to look at the white walls and lawns from a distance, with a puckered and oddly casual expression, from which nobody would have guessed that he was thinking:

"What the devil shall I do with the place?"

For he had decided that a war was coming, and that he was going home, and that United Players might sue and be damned. They did announce that intention on 10 August and they were. The sum they claimed was about £18,000.

Had he been asked what he gave up in Hollywood, his son Ronald thought he would probably have answered irritably: "Nothing at all," and added upon reflection, "though they always paid me extremely well."

"I am tired of being a star in Hollywood," he told reporters as he boarded the *Aquitania* in New York on 23 August. When asked what his next picture would be he said:

"I am making a British film next: 'The Man Who Lost Himself'."[3]

On that 23 August Sir Nevile Henderson in Berlin was going through the last painful efforts to avert war. The Swedish go-between, Birger Dahlerus, was mixing in with amateur enthusiasm, and the officials of the Wilhelmstrasse were politely washing their hands. For a man who intended to take part in war propaganda, Leslie could not have timed his return better.

The crossing to England was uneventful, though not without a qualm for Leslie, for the gipsies had once told him that he would die by water, and he had a strong reverence for the supernatural.

By the time the liner docked in Southampton he had worked out the beginnings of a war programme for himself. He would make films with a patriotic purpose. He would broadcast to America. He would give an impulse to British propaganda. To his ambitions in all this there were no limits, and even today there comes a catch in the throat when we read this extract from his first wartime broadcast to America:

> I can't explain the mystery of the call that comes to people from the land of their birth – I don't have to explain it to you, anyway. The call of Britain seems particularly potent, doesn't it? – look at the way they've come hurrying in response from the four corners of the earth – especially as that call comes at what must be the most critical moment of our whole long history. Most of you, I'm sure, will know what I mean when I speak of the curious elation which comes from sharing in a high and mysterious destiny. The destiny of Britain we cannot know for certain, but we can guess at it, and pray for it, and work towards it as we find ourselves singled out of all the nations of the world for the rare honour of fighting alone against the huge and ruthless forces of tyranny.
>
> There's a great thrill in all that, believe me, as there's a thrill in observing at close quarters the enormous preparations for

defence. One notices it particularly in a country town such as I
live near. Never have there been so many soldiers in this island.
I swear there's more battledress than civilian clothes. And such
a variety of soldiers. The townsfolk are bewildered by soldiers
from Quebec speaking an unfamiliar French, soldiers with vital
accents from Toronto, wild and gigantic soldiers from
Queensland wearing large romantic hats, quiet soldiers from
New Zealand with Boy Scout hats, and soldiers with the voices
of every shire of Britain; not to mention the men of Norway,
Poland, Czechoslovakia, Holland, Belgium – yes, and French
soldiers, too, many of them, moving freely about in the one place
left in Europe where they can hold up their heads and know they
are still in the war against the common enemy. And up and down
the High Street all day long stream the convoys, artillery, tanks,
motor transports, Red Cross, staff cars, motor cyclists. And in
all our history our countryside never looked like this, dotted all
over with trenches, machine-gun emplacements, block-houses,
pillboxes, concrete shelters, tank-traps, landmines. One feels
that the quiet villages of England are the focal point of the world
– as indeed they are, for they are in the front line of the battle
for freedom. And one gets a kick out of being in that front line
– you must confess you would too.

Chapter 5

The War with Goebbels

The Whitehall official looked across his desk and asked: "So you want to make films in this country in wartime?" "That's it."

Outside on the wet, dark streets of October 1939 a few taxis crawled past, their cowled headlamps scarcely striking a reflection off the dark macadam. The lights of Europe, though not entirely out, were effectively dimmed. A girl secretary was carefully stretching the thick blackout curtains across a sandbagged window.

"Under these conditions?"

"I don't see why not."

"Noel Coward has taken an important liaison job in Paris with the French Government on enemy propaganda. You'd do a job of that sort very well."

"I want to make films here," said Howard quietly.

"Couldn't you make them in Hollywood? The Americans think the world of you."

"I've just come from Hollywood. They couldn't make the kind of films that I want to make."

"Oh, and what have you in view?" The official sat back and joined his fingertips.

"The first film that I want to make is a documentary of the British White Paper on the outbreak of war. I want to put it out as a film record, using some newsreel stuff, but acting the real parts. There is a theme I want to bring home. Let me explain – I am working on a simple principle: that the mind will always triumph over brute force in the long run. We must bring that out in our war film. And at the same time we must show them what Nazism is like."

"But acting what parts ...?"

"Oh, acting Hitler, for a start, and then I want to play Sir Nevile Henderson myself.[1] The last bid for peace against the tactics of Ribbentrop."

The civil servant stroked his chin thoughtfully.

"I must say, Mr Howard, that if you are going to act the part of a British Ambassador, we shall have to ask the Foreign Office and get the permission of Lord Halifax."

"Well, will you do that? You see, nobody abroad wants to read official documents now. They won't buy your White Paper. But they will crowd into the cinemas to see an official documentary."

"I suppose we can apply, but there's an awful lot of obstacles that perhaps you don't realise to making films now. There is of course rationing. Manpower, material, petrol are all rationed. You will want equipment, telephones, accommodation, technicians, actors, and extras. We are trying to get organised to fight a war. We've never yet been awfully successful at making films here in peacetime, and to start now in wartime seems crazy to me."

"Just for that reason, because it seems crazy, I think it may succeed."

Lord Halifax was duly consulted, and looked puzzled. It was certainly a novel idea to put a British Ambassador on the screen, but did Mr Howard quite realise the state of mind in which Sir Nevile had returned from his Berlin ordeal? Göring, Ribbentrop, and Hitler had been altogether too much for this ailing man, who had gone away to Rauceby and was certain to die soon of cancer. His Lordship demurred, and finally put his veto on the project, but that was a year later.

In this he had an ally in Leslie Howard's own partner and scriptwriter, Anatole de Grunwald. The practical mind of Grunwald tempered some of the higher inspirations of Leslie Howard. Of

Russian birth, more a man of the world than Leslie, he could see that the obstacles were not worth climbing.

"Listen, Leslie; Sir Nevile made a failure of it, and no matter what you believe in, you can't make a successful film about failure. Let's think up some kind of a modern Pimpernel who sees war coming, has a brush with the Germans, and gets across the ideas that you want."

Out of these talks the idea of Pimpernel Smith was born, the absentminded professor who manages to fool the Nazis.

They had formed a company – Two-Cities Films Ltd. – to make the Leslie Howard productions. They took into a directorship for his business skill, a chartered accountant with a wide practice in the theatrical and film world, and moved out to Denham Studios in Buckinghamshire with the blessing of the Films Section of the Ministry of Information. But it was only in October 1940, a year after his first conversations in Whitehall on making a film about the origins of the war, that work on 'Pimpernel Smith' could begin.

Meanwhile Leslie had found many other things to do. He was over in France in January 1940 to discuss the idea of a Film Entente, to pool production and distribution.

In April 1940 – the last days of the 'phoney war' – he was in London for the first night of 'Gone with the Wind'.

"If you sneeze, you miss my part," he smiled to the critics.

He joined an Ideas Committee in the Ministry of Information, he broadcast to America about the war, he wrote articles for the British Press, and he listened attentively to a new voice on the air – that of a renegade Englishman named William Joyce,[2] who was broadcasting in English from Germany and had earned himself, by his carefully-schooled accent, the name of Lord Haw-Haw. Leslie found time for all these things, even time to write a serious article on the subject of Union with America.

How would you like to be a perpetual exile? How would you like to be a person who is divided between two countries in such a way that, whichever of the two he finds himself in for any length of time, he must invariably feel himself exiled from the other? Well, I am that particular kind of exile. Let me explain:

After world war number one, I felt a great urge to put a considerable distance between myself and the cursed continent of Europe. I was obliged to part from my native land.

I went to live in the United States, technically a foreign country, in which I was technically an alien. No foreign country could have been more hospitable to a poor immigrant. It permitted me to work, to prosper, to raise a family, to find friends, to enjoy life.

They even laughed at the English humour. It made me realise in a very few weeks that in actual fact I was not in a foreign country. As the years went by this feeling became implicit and profound. My friends wondered why I did not become an American citizen: somehow I could not persuade myself to do that.

I have been in Britain since the start of the war and though it would be hard to pull myself away in these dynamic days, the pull from my almost native America is very, very strong.

How idiotic it is that these great and enlightened peoples must still regard each other politically as foreigners!

Why can we not unite into a great federation reaching the four corners of the earth and spanning and controlling the oceans? Here's my vote for the Great Union, in war and in peace, for the benefit of the world and the safety of humanity.

When the lull in the West ended, and the campaign rolled on to the glory and disaster of Dunkirk, Leslie was down at the Channel ports meeting survivors, interviewing a French sergeant, one of those who had been sunk by the German Luftwaffe in the Channel when returning home to France and rescued by the Royal Navy.

"The ship was a French merchant ship, carrying out the terms of the armistice: the Germans were informed of its passage across the Channel; the ship was brilliantly lit."

It gave him the idea for another talk to America. On 25 August 1940, he broadcast on the meaning of Dunkirk.

All over the world today, but particularly in the zone of war, men are consciously or unconsciously discovering for themselves a great fundamental truth. They are finding out what it is in life they hold most dear.

A strange and wonderful light has been thrown on this subject by members of the French fighting forces, who found themselves in Britain or escaped to it after the tragic collapse of their Fatherland.

Then he related the fate of those whose exile was so much more desperate than his own. His scripts could not vie with the heights and depths of the Churchill rhetoric, but they told a simple clear story and they were widely heard in America.

"I have been broadcasting week after week for many months to the United States and the Empire," he wrote of it from Denham in March 1941, "and the essence of my views as regards the enemy is to fight them to the last ditch."

In this turmoil the making of his films began. To be near his work he rented a roomy country house close to Denham, and there the directors and actors lived together an exciting and unpunctual life: Leslie Howard, Anatole de Grunwald, Irene Howard, Valerie

Hobson, Violette Cunnington, a brilliant young studio secretary whom Leslie had discovered during the filming of 'Pygmalion' with Gabriel Pascal in 1937. Violette with much competence managed his studio work, acting as liaison between him and the outside world.

Violette plays only a minor role in this story, and she is suddenly and dramatically removed from the scene by untimely death. But many who had dealings with the team of talent that produced the Howard wartime films remember her somewhat strident voice with a slight French intonation, the keen, vivacious expression, the intense blue eyes, and light brown hair of the studio secretary.

"Leslee, Leslee!" she used to look up from the telephone to remind him of some appointment he had forgotten, and every day he seemed to forget something.

Perhaps undue notice has been drawn to Violette by a bequest in his will leaving her the house in Beverly Hills,[3] though she did not survive to receive it. It was natural for Leslie to be surrounded by a galaxy of beautiful women. They stirred his imagination on and off the set. He watched them in their parts, comparing the heroines of the drama with the women whom he met in real life.

"A man in love is a stupid thing," he once mused, sitting in a deck chair in the sunshine of his Dorking home. "He bores you stiff in real life or anywhere else. Romeo acquires something in his later scenes, interesting in his tragic moments like a kind of adolescent Hamlet.

"But a woman in love is fascinating. She has a kind of aura. Shakespeare was obviously fascinated by Juliet, and it was the woman that he enriched."

At the weekend, as if tired of basking in this splendour of ladies, he disappeared silently from Denham, to the house at Westcott, to unspan with his family from the mad film world and dip into a book on the lawn.

Nobody sitting comfortably in a cinema today and seeing one of those films played over can realise quite how they were made, and in what a hectic atmosphere the obstacles were met and overcome.

After 'Pimpernel Smith' – and that made people laugh at a time when there was little to laugh about – there was 'The 49th Parallel'. Its theme was the indoctrinated crew of a wrecked U-boat escaping across Canada and spreading their *Kultur* as they went. But what an operation to get the cast across the Atlantic in wartime! Once there, one of the principal ladies opted for the American continent and stayed there. She had subsequently to be replaced.

Back to Denham to finish the film with a new leading lady. Overlapping '49th Parallel' came the great idea of 'The First of the Few'. Leslie was approached with a proposal to film the life of R. J. Mitchell, the aircraft designer, who laboured in the face of official indifference to produce the aircraft that won the Battle of Britain. He decided to take the rôle of Mitchell himself, and sought the help of Fighter Command.

There was a goulash luncheon early in 1941 at the Hungarian 'Csarda' restaurant in Soho with an Air Ministry film liaison officer, a short, tubby officer with twinkling blue eyes and the medal ribbons of the First World War. Leslie was accompanied by Violette Cunnington, who listened to all the business conversations.

"Very charming, slim, nice features, oval face, very intelligent," the RAF man recollected her clearly years afterwards. "I tried to concentrate on explaining the difficulties of getting Fighter co-operation."

"Mr Howard, I am just trying to tell you what we're up against, even though the Air Ministry supports you to the full. If the Commander-in-Chief decides he can't spare you a 'plane, you won't get it. I'll be surprised if you get one Spitfire out of the brass for 'The First of the Few'.

"Let me tell you what happened over 'Target for Tonight'. We wanted one Wellington bomber to film in – they wouldn't give me one. I couldn't even get the bits. When there was a crash I used to tear over to see if I could get the wreckage.

"But even the old wrecks were being cannibalised. In the end I got a nacelle from Nottingham and a Wellington rump from the Home Counties. We joined them together with painted cloth, and that was the Wellington bomber that starred in 'Target for Tonight'."

Leslie went into the story of R. J. Mitchell rather more deeply than is usual for a film director. The official material was dry, the story of the widow insufficient, but through a determined young woman in the theatrical world whom he met by pure chance over a drink in London, he found himself whisked out into the country and introduced to one of the Vickers' top scientists, then working on cathode-ray tubes and other scientific advances. They sat and talked for hours. From him he heard the amazing story of Mitchell, the £6-a-week draughtsman who became absorbed in aerodynamics and studied the shape of birds in flight in his search for the plane that could outfly the new fighters that Germany would build. Mitchell lying on his back on a clifftop and watching the wings of seagulls floating past.

Leslie heard also of incredible delays in Whitehall, before it was realised that there was genius in Mitchell, of an official minute written on his proposals: "This man must be mad", of stupidity and perhaps worse in the Contracts Branch of the Air Ministry.

In fact, so alarmed did Mr Neville Chamberlain become at the thoroughness with which Leslie Howard was studying his subject, that although he was no longer Prime Minister, he thought it prudent to write a directive on certain aspects of the story that he deemed best should remain secret, and so they did. There must have been twinges in the conscience of Neville Chamberlain.[4]

Yet the story never ceased to harass the sensitive mind of Leslie Howard, he being much more than a director of films, and some of the delays that held up work on his films were caused by that inquiring trait, when an aspect of the story occurred to him that the cinema public would not understand or, if it did, would certainly not appreciate.

So by degrees the difficulties were overcome, and they were worth overcoming this time. The new Chief of Fighter Command, Sholto Douglas, once the first heat of the Battle of Britain had died down, found it possible to let the film company work with operational squadrons. Sholto Douglas found him an operational wing at Iddesleigh in Hampshire where, with the support of David Niven, much of the filming was done.

The most famous fighter pilots of the war – Bader, Cunningham, Townsend – came into the filming of 'The First of the Few'. They flew, they acted, they advised; unpaid. All Leslie could do to repay them was to invite them as his guests to the Savoy Hotel. They celebrated the completion of the film with a party at Fighter Command Headquarters in August 1942, just before the Dieppe raid; took off to give air cover to that, and returned, fewer than before, but casual, charming – very like Leslie himself, though, being a modest sort of man, he would not have thought of that. Blood, sweat, and tears went to its making, and when the final scene was devised Leslie turned to Anatole de Grunwald and said:

"I want here just a touch of the supernatural. Mitchell's bird of omen was the seagull. He loved them and studied them. So when he is dying in the garden, don't show the death itself, just put in a shot of a gull hovering past, and as she sees it passing, his wife suddenly understands that he is gone."

With this mystic incident, they sealed the last episode of 'The First of the Few'.

Chapter 6

The Bristol Story

Civil flying had to go on, even at the height of the Battle of Britain. It had begun to become indispensable to the life and business of the Western world. Moreover, sea travel to Europe had suddenly stopped, and that made it imperative to open the Lisbon air route again as soon as it could be done, and with whatever aircraft could be found to fly it.

The fugitive pilots and aircraft from Europe were sorted and graded. Eight Sabena aircraft arrived from Belgium, which would be useful on the Congo routes. Of the Dutch, *Aigrette* and *Curlew* came in next, with *King Falcon* from Lisbon, and *Buzzard* and *Heron* from Naples. These planes and their pilots were precious at that moment. The DC-3 machines were among the most modern available in 1940. The Dutch pilots all spoke English. They operated and wrote their flight reports in English, the language of international flying. It was natural, then, to keep aircraft and crews together on whatever links they could maintain with the Continent.

There were only two that could still be operated. The long line to Stockholm lay over territory occupied by the enemy. That must be flown to bring in Swedish ball bearings, vital to British war production. It was a route to be flown at great heights by night in peril of enemy radar interception and night fighters; it demanded high navigational performances and the closest contacts with the RAF. Several types of aircraft were tried. De Havilland Mosquitoes flew it best, sometimes with odd passengers cramped into the bomb bays. A hazardous run, and the pilots chosen for it were taken from British airlines.

This left the Lisbon line. The new Dutch wing of BOAC was best equipped to fly it. Their DC–3 aircraft seemed ideal for that distance. A protective belt of sea would lie between them and the French coast, making daylight flying possible. So the decision was taken on principle between Civil Aviation Branch of the Air Ministry and the Dutch Government in exile that KLM machines and pilots would fly the Lisbon route. It was partly served by BOAC flying-boats on the Empire routes from Plymouth to the Middle East and Africa, landing on the Tagus, but a regular daily line from London to Lisbon was highly desirable too.

As the pilots were released by degrees from military service and clearing camps, A. E. Johnson, their English manager, mustered them and collected passport photographs. He showed them to me years later. They lie before me as I write. The laughter of those 1934 days when Parmentier flew the Melbourne Air Race was gone from their faces in 1940. Turning over these pictures today, I see the reflection in their eyes of that ordeal of fire and steel that had just overwhelmed their country. Even the wireless operator, Cornelis van Brugge, the jester of the party, wore for once a solemn expression.

The senior pilots came together again, with Parmentier in charge as Flying Superintendent. He chose Quirinus Tepas and Theo Verhoeven to make the first flights on the London–Lisbon route. Johnson found a crew office in the buildings of Heston airport. There, within the network of the London anti-aircraft batteries, with balloon barrages to eastward and rough poles and scaffolding being pile-driven in the meadows against German troop-carriers and gliders, the London–Lisbon venture began.

Quirinus Tepas flew the opening flight from London. A British pilot, Jimmy Weir of BOAC, flew with him as First Officer. Engbertus Rosevink was the flight engineer, and Cornelis van

Brugge the radio operator. They took the *Ibis* on 25 July and flew her from Heston to Oporto and so on to Lisbon. A primitive code was arranged to tell them whether the weather conditions and the state of the blitz would allow them to return next day.

"Q.G.O. – you may return; Q.G.N. – remain where you are."

The direct route was 1,001 miles, but it would have taken them over the Cherbourg peninsula and Brittany, within easy range of Messerschmitt and Junkers fighters. So they flew west over Exeter and down the Bristol Channel, leaving Lundy Island on the starboard wing, and then south-westerly to pass over the Isles of Scilly; finally south-south-west on latitude 7 towards the Spanish peninsula. This course took them in a wide arc away from danger. Apart from navigational problems it was an uneventful flight, but at Lisbon, Weir took over security guard. He carried a pistol; for nobody knew what tricks the Germans might use to get possession of these aircraft. The German Lufthansa office was right across the passage from the British BOAC offices at Sintra airport; the German mechanics had access to the tarmac when they serviced Lufthansa airliners. There were risks of sabotage, but the return flight of 26 July was without incident either, and so was the night in Lisbon, where the crew stayed in the Hotel Europa. No German agent approached them, though the arrival of the Dutchmen must have been noticed.

Flights went well till the tenth day, when there was low cloud and poor visibility over England, and the homing *Buzzard* was given a wrong bearing from Exeter radio station. It was not safe to be off course in low visibility approaching the defences of Great Britain in 1940, with gun crews ready to repel invasion at any moment and shoot at unidentified aircraft.

Weir noted this error. Verhoeven flying on 10 August and Tepas on the 11th observed that there was a radio beacon on the Scillies giving bearings for the RAF. "Why can't we use that too?" they said.

Next day in Parmentier's office in Heston the Dutch air captains gathered with the British co-pilots and the wireless operators who had flown the Lisbon route. As they talked about flying conditions, outside on the Heston tarmac Hurricanes stood by for combat.

"It seems," said Parmentier, "that there's a set of RAF radio beacons on the South Coast. We should be able to use them too. We should be told about them."

"Contact Air Ministry," advised the co-pilots.

"We picked up the Scillies at an adequate distance to take bearings," said Verhoeven, "but they may change their timing and wavelengths from week to week."

"We ought to be kept informed of that."

"Why not ask to have all bearings passed through one station? Poole is the most powerful. Let Poole keep in constant touch with the aircraft, and pass on bearings from Whitchurch too."

"Can someone shake up Exeter, Parmentier?"

"We want a short-wave radio beacon like this one at Heston," said Tepas, "especially during winter flying."

"And what about flying conditions? The Luftwaffe was over Weymouth and Portland yesterday. See anything, Tepas?"

"Nothing at all," said Tepas thoughtfully, as he sat and traced his course on the map table. "But with never knowing what goes on, and with flak and fighters about, don't we need to know minimum conditions for flying?"

"Say a thousand-feet ceiling with one-and-a-quarter miles visibility – not less. We need that to operate safely."

"And the Lisbon route itself?" Parmentier asked.

The pilots sipped their tea. Slowly Tepas spoke, pointing to the map:

"A bit close to Ushant at that point."

"Is that the general feeling?"

"Yes, it is."

"Suggestions?"

"With the range of a DC-3 on present payload, run from a point ten degrees West of Cape Villano on a course to Foynes radio station. Stay west of the Scillies – then take a bearing on Lundy and up the Bristol Channel."

"You could stage at Bristol."

"You could indeed. We may even have to move the whole outfit to Bristol if this goes on."

"You might have to, with a headwind, or land even farther west – say Chivenor."

"Couldn't we make use of Foynes?" asked the Dutch air captains, and Parmentier looked up from his minute book at the British co-pilots:

"What's wrong with landing in Éire?"

"I wouldn't say it would help awfully much, Parmentier," said one of the British pilots. "Better land at Oporto on the way home. That will give you fuel for another two hundred miles flying."

"And what about the Lisbon end?"

"I had a look round in Lisbon," said Cornelis van Brugge. "These damn Germans see us come and go. Here I have my tin hat to comfort me, and I take it on board with me. But all the same, it's best if the Germans don't always know when we leave."

"Yes, Dirk, we should vary the days of flying, and the hours of departure too."

"Why not take off two hours before sunrise? Then we pass Ushant in darkness."

"And shorten the route?"

"That could be considered – in winter, anyway."

"And let's have Air Ministry get us a fixed call sign from Oporto to give us a bearing there."

"So, we want more beacons. We want the route as far west as possible. We want to vary the schedules."

The pilots trooped out of the Heston conference, leaving Parmentier with the map and his notes. He summarised, reported, and the route on the Oporto–Foynes bearing, extending to 10° West, was adopted. On that route they would fly the Lisbon line for the next four years.

But three days later the great daylight blitz broke on London. The Battle of Britain pilots and air defence accounted for seventy-six enemy aircraft. Plainly a regular air service from Heston to Lisbon could not be maintained under those conditions. On the 18th, Göring's men were back by daylight and lost seventy-one machines. Then came the switch to night bombing and the long pounding nights of the London blitz. So began Operation WESTWARD HO! British Overseas Airways Corporation moved westwards away from the blitz. The Dutch wing was moved, on 20 September, out of Heston to Whitchurch aerodrome south of Bristol, the equipment and stores following by road. Heston was left to RAF Fighter Command.

The pilots flew ahead with the machines, and Johnson motored across England with some of the Dutch ground staff and a carload of wireless apparatus. The Home Guard saw them pass with suspicion and reported their guttural talk to the Wiltshire Constabulary. For the roadblocks were up, the signposts were down, and the Home Guard were watching for cars with radio sets in them, for bicyclists with foreign accents, for musicians with heavy violin cases, for tramps with duelling scars on their cheeks, for nuns wearing field-service boots.

They reached Bristol and drove on southwards to the airport at Whitchurch. No more than a field with two hangars and one runway. Dundry Hill, a natural obstacle of 450 feet, did not improve it. The

Mendip Hills came altogether too close. Round two sides of the airfield there were rows of houses, rather like the surroundings of Croydon. An old stone farmhouse nearby, elm trees and hedged pastures. A concrete-and-glass control tower with Standard beam approach, the runway just 1,000 yards of concrete. Weather reports from Gloucester. A teleprinter service from the Air Ministry in London. A telephone link with BOAC offices in the Grand Spa Hotel in Bristol. A local bus service.

"With a cross wind, Quirinus, you'd have to take off here over the grass. What a small office they've given us!"

And so to find billets in Bristol for twenty-five Dutch airmen and twelve ground staff. The Station Superintendent hurried through the offices of Bristol estate agents, to find that housing property in the West country was much sought after at that time. But by knocking at doors himself, he at length found room for them all.

Then he bent his patience to the business of their status. Could a Dutchman ride a bicycle to Bridewell police station in 1940? Aliens were forbidden by Home Office regulations to have bicycles, but how else could these aliens report regularly to the Police Station, as the Home Office required? The crews and ground staff could not choose their time. They must be servicing aircraft and flying aircraft on urgent Government business.

The Bristol police were perplexed. What! Aliens flying aircraft in 1940, and handling Air Ministry codes, but not allowed to ride bicycles? Sergeant, some notepaper! Make out bicycle permits for these —— flying Dutchmen.

The first day of operations from Whitchurch brought a sad mishap. Quirinus Tepas was to take an aircraft empty from Whitchurch to Heston, pick up passengers there and fly on to Lisbon. But on 21 September Heston reported fog and low visibility. Tepas in Whitchurch was anxious and fretting to start. His passengers were waiting in London. It was the first flight from the new base, and he did not want it postponed.

"I'll come over and take a look, to see if it's all right," he told Heston.

Tepas took off in the hope that the weather would lift. The *Heron* flew over Heston, and he talked down to the control-tower. The weather was worse than before and the ceiling too low for safety. Peering about for what he took to be the airfield, Tepas came low over a grass field, lost height, and taxied straight into one of the invasion poles. There were no casualties, except the *Heron*. She was a total write-off. The beautiful *Heron*, the valuable *Heron*.

"You think you'll take a look," shouted Parmentier, "and see what the weather's like. And what happens? Now we have only five aircraft to run the Lisbon line."

Then came administrative trouble. More Dutch pilots were released from military service for civil flying. The Lisbon line could be flown with all-Dutch crews, if the Air Ministry would consent. Or would it insist on its British security guards? This argument kept the little fleet grounded for several weeks until Parmentier got his way, as he usually did.

The blitz moved nearer in November 1940, as if chasing them westwards: first Amsterdam, then London, now Bristol. The Luftwaffe came in across the Channel, striking at Plymouth, Exeter, Bristol. It attacked Whitchurch on a Sunday night, 24 November. The sirens started just before six, and the droning of bombers was heard. At six o'clock parachute flares, chandelier flares, incendiaries, and lastly the big stuff. Airliners stood parked about the airport. Seventy bombs fell near by, twenty within the perimeter. The pilots sat in the air-raid shelter and played spoof. When they emerged they could see that it was the inferno of Schiphol all over again. A British Ensign airliner and the *Curlew* were going up in flames.

"There goes *Curlew*, boys! Now we have only four aircraft to run the Lisbon line."

Bombs hit the centre of Bristol, they hit the docks, they even hit the dogs. Bristol greyhound stadium was hit by high explosives, the kennels wrecked, and the greyhounds set loose: fleeting shadows of panic as they raced through the glare of fires and the darkness of the blackout. The raiders ceased to drone overhead by 10 pm. For once old Chilcott, the post-office telephonist at Whitchurch control tower, got leave to go home. It was his one day off in eight months of sixteen hours a day at the switchboard. At Hazelbury Road he found his roof and front door blown off, and his wife and daughter still crouched under the stairs.

The fires that the Luftwaffe had lit in Bristol were still burning next day. The streets were blocked with rubble. Johnson took his car and tried to reach Bristol so that he could find out whether his flying personnel were among the casualties. It took three hours to drive the three miles into the city through the blocked streets. Quirinus Tepas got out and walked round Clifton knocking up the Dutch crews one by one. There were no casualties among them in the eight big raids that Bristol suffered.

Air-raid wardens and police sometimes came across one or other of the crews toiling among the rubble with the Bristol folk, and paused with suspicion at their slow, slightly guttural talk, before realising that these were the Dutch airmen from Whitchurch. They got to recognise Cornelis van Brugge sitting with his tin hat in the Mauretania bar, waiting for fire-watching duty.

On 17 December flights to Lisbon were resumed, with the four remaining aircraft – *King Falcon, Aigrette, Buzzard,* and *Ibis.* Quirinus Tepas took his crew out to the *Ibis* – de Koning the co-pilot, Rosevink the engineer/steward, Cornelis van Brugge the wireless operator; gripping his tin hat.

They had been briefed about the radio beacons. They had been given the call signs and codes they required.

The British had given them their entire trust. The Lisbon line was now theirs to fly. *Ibis* rose, dipped her wing over Dundry Hill, and set her course south-west down the Bristol Channel that December day for 10° West and Lisbon.

Thereafter, life in the West country took on a certain pattern. The Admiralty worked from Bath, the Ministry of Civil Aviation from Bristol. With a safe air-raid shelter under the Clifton Rock, reached through a tunnel in the ballroom, BOAC worked in the Spa Hotel. It mustered the passengers in the Grand Hotel. That was the hotel of the 'Outward Bound'. It was an eerie sensation to part there for nobody knew how long.

Times of aircraft departure and arrival and the name of the airport were kept secret from passengers. Next of kin could accompany them no further than the lounge of the Grand Hotel. There the comely girls of Bristol came to meet the pilots. There wives and husbands and lovers parted. There the courier checked his lists and noted next of kin, and mustered the passengers for the airport bus. The girl with titian hair at the desk of the Grand Hotel saw a lot that went on in the war, both of gladness and grief.

When Whitchurch had got the bugs out of itself, famous and important people came down to fly through. There goes Prince Bernhard to the United States, and here comes Admiral Syfrett from Gibraltar, Crown Princess Martha of Norway, the Duke of Palmela flying home to report to his Government in Lisbon, the Duke of Alba flying to report to General Franco, Sir Samuel and Lady Hoare arriving, with butler, from the Madrid Embassy and flying on by Flamingo to London. (The butler particularly impressed the ground staff at Whitchurch.) Then Sir Ronald Campbell, British Ambassador in Lisbon, and with him Sir Cosmo Parkinson. Then in reverse the butler – *quel grand seigneur!* Sir Sam and Lady Hoare flying out to Lisbon for Spain. In October 1942 "an awful flap" when Mrs Roosevelt was expected in and double guards were mounted at Whitchurch. A corps of gentlemen came down from London to meet her, and in the same month there was a visit by a very erect old lady from Badminton. Queen Mary took tea in the airport mess and wrote the airport manager "a very nice letter expressing her thanks" two days later. It had been so interesting to see how civil flying was conducted in wartime!

All this lay ahead when the Lisbon airliners began to fly again in December 1940.

"For Christ's sake, Quirinus, that bloody hill comes up at us every time like a charging elephant."

And Dundry beacon had just that effect on anyone in the cockpit as the *Ibis* came towards the end of the runway at take-off.

"Well, shut the bulkhead door, Cornelis. There's no need to worry my passengers too."

Chapter 7

Lisbon Scene

In opening the Lisbon line a spy-line into England was reopened too. The Germans need no longer rely on parachutes and rubber boats landing scared men and women with imperfect English in country districts. Instead, from Lisbon they would be able to slip neutral agents past the British Consular officials on the pretext of essential business. They would be able to fly them in comfort to the West country, and use the neutral diplomatic bag to get their reports out of London to the German Embassy in Lisbon. They might even be able to get precious contraband too on this route – iridium, uranium, diamonds.

Things had already happened on this line in wartime. It had from the start been a link with a neutral country. During the early days of war the clearing of passengers had sometimes taken longer than the flight from Amsterdam; but after a week or so, quiet, unobtrusive officials came down to the airport and set a new system going. Then clearance went smoothly and fast again. Passengers did not feel that they were being held back or watched. Even the girl with the extra passport in her luggage felt no undue concern. She did not know that the Customs officer caught a glimpse of the mottled green cover of a German passport as he went lightly through her dressing-case. And quietly the Immigration Officer, looking at the date-stamps in her British passport, asked when she was last in Germany, memorised her answer, and said nothing. She was passed through the airport to the coach. When her heart ceased to beat so fast and she felt that all was well again, then she was being watched with a purpose for the first time.

Just that mistake of packing a second passport instead of carrying it – that and an evasive answer to a question. The man who followed her speculatively down Jermyn Street had more in mind than usually preoccupies men who follow girls down Jermyn Street. What office was she visiting there? And whom? One spy leads to another. The first mistake leads to the second.

For other reasons, too, Lisbon was the heart of the espionage game. From Portuguese Angola it was possible to get industrial diamonds out of Johannesburg, and a small packet taken from Lisbon docks to the Lusitania Express for Madrid meant a lot to the German war effort. Portugal itself, with its mineral wealth, was an object of interest, and the Secret Services of all powers would watch wolfram[1] production and outbid each other to get this precious stuff for the hardening of steel.

All European nationalities would filter into the brightly lit cafes of Lisbon, exchange intelligence, and move on. Rumours would be sown for the purpose of deception, escape routes out of Europe would end there. Everybody who came and went would be under scrutiny, not merely by the Portuguese, but by the agents of the warring Powers and their neutral friends.

At first it was only the hazards of the route that preoccupied Tepas and his crew.

"Chivenor below us now, Quirinus."

The *Ibis* flew on steadily west.

"Lundy Island on the starboard wing."

Ibis turned 7° West. They found the Foynes–Oporto bearing at 50° North and turned almost due south. The long run south on longitude 10° West had begun. The sky, lightly overcast, was empty of aircraft. Four hours later de Koning called across:

"Passing Oporto."

Seven hours after take-off she was circling over the Tagus, over the white walls and red roofs of Lisbon, to touch down on Sintra airfield.[2] There was no concrete runway at all, and after rain had made a morass of the hard earth it was not easy landing. The airport buildings were small and primitive. Allied and enemy pilots were apt to bump into each other as they walked through the swing doors into the reception hall. Their offices faced each other across the floor.

The British, with their command of the sea, had a flying-boat service as well as the Bristol-Lisbon route. Empire flying-boats of the C-class came down in the estuary of the Tagus, made fast to moorings, and discharged their mail and passengers at Cabo Ruivo jetty. The fishermen looked up from mending their nets and watched them alight and take off in a flurry of spray.

They carried the official documents of four continents. From Africa, India, Australia, and Asia came the diplomatic, military, and Colonial Office mailbags. Sometimes 200 sacks at a time would be handled by the British Embassy guards in and out of the vans that plied up and down from the Embassy strong room to the waterfront.

The flying-boats took six tons at a time, as they surged off again for the United Kingdom or West Africa. Their flying instructions came to them in sealed envelopes with weather reports and other information from the British Embassy secret information room. From a compact diplomatic mission the Embassy had become a large traffic and intelligence directorate for the Empire at war. It had more than 300 personnel with Consular staff, issuing Navicerts[3] to neutral shipping, watching Axis spies and blockade runners.

The staff of the air attaché, Wing Commander Jack Schreiber, was increased by meteorological experts and communications officers to maintain cipher touch with Gibraltar and London. Intelligence and security men were thick among the diplomatic and consular personnel. *Ibis* was met by the British traffic manager and his staff, Basto, Brito, and Bonito, the Portuguese servants of the company.

Wherever there were mailbags to move, passenger lists to check, cargoes to clear, schedules to announce, reservations to book, they were there with glistening smiles and watchful eyes. They knew and noted the movements of Axis agents about the airport. They foresaw difficulties, they acted, waited about, they smiled all the time. They grinned with delight at the crew of the *Ibis*.

"The Portuguese Security Police are asking questions about your crew," said Herbert Recknell, the manager. "Just stay about, if you don't mind."

"Sure we'll stay about, Mr Recknell."

It was said that the Portuguese Security Police had some special links with Admiral Canaris of the German Intelligence Service. To begin with, their attitude to the Dutch pilots was markedly suspicious.

Tepas and his crew sat in the restaurant and waited. At last they were cleared and the *Ibis* was cleared. The Portuguese security guard took over for the night. Quirinus and his crew were free to enter Lisbon, to have dinner, and to post letters home.

Nobody who has not made the Lisbon run in wartime knows that dazzling contrast. From the drizzle and blackout of wartime England, with ration cards, queues, secrecy, and security posters, the breadth and glitter of the Avenida da Liberdade and the big square Pedro IV. Everywhere a sheen of light. The palm and acacia trees shone in it; and the cosmopolitan cafe life of Lisbon sat and wondered about the war at a safe distance.

"Psst! Mister! I buy pound notes at feefty escudos. I sell you five-pound notes for two hundred feefty!"

They walked into their favourite cafe, the Parisienne, and ordered drinks. It was a place where you could eat a snack and sit about all evening meeting friends. On the wall a photograph of the Portuguese Premier Salazar looked thoughtful about neutrality.

"All very good. A very quiet run," said Cornelis van Brugge, watching the girls strolling past outside.

"Do you think those are Germans over there, Cornelis?"

"Maybe. We needn't worry."

Sometimes Quirinus Tepas had the impression of being watched as they sat at dinner, or of being followed as they strolled the streets of Lisbon after dark. But who followed them? Was it the British, the Germans, or the Portuguese? It was difficult to know. Who would watch a Dutch civil pilot out at night in Lisbon in the second year of the war?

The German Ambassador, Baron Hoyningen-Huene,[4] had his swollen diplomatic staff too. Spy and counterspy! Two intelligence officers of the German Military Security Service – Colonel von Karsthof, and his deputy, Captain Fritz Cramer – were active about Lisbon. These two officers watched the Dutch airliners with speculative eyes. What brought cargoes out must take cargoes back. If passengers came out, passengers could return to England. Portuguese newsagents received orders from the German Embassy for a wide range of British daily newspapers, scientific and medical journals, and trade magazines. The freight carried on the Lisbon run increased. There were times when they piled the newspapers on the empty passenger seats.[5]

On the homeward run there was a waiting list for England: those from the occupied countries of Europe who could find their way past the Vichy police and the Spanish frontier guards and were accepted by the Passport and Visa officials of the British Consulate General; fugitives from Hitler, stranded tourists, businessmen, and a few priority travellers among the Spaniards and Portuguese. There were also British officials on His Majesty's business, and a few British travellers of robust appearance, and obviously of military age, sporting handlebar moustaches and improbably dressed in grey flannels and hacking jackets. Officers in transit to and from the Middle East.

This traffic was noted and reported to Admiral Wilhelm Canaris in Berlin. The German Chief of Intelligence went furtively to Lisbon and conferred with Baron Hoyningen-Huene. The German Ambassador told me after the war that they agreed against sabotage of ships or aircraft as being the most risky, wasteful, and least effective form of secret service warfare. But Canaris had ideas that the Lisbon line deserved his attention in other ways – he could use it for his own purposes.

Once or twice in Lisbon cafes a stranger would cross over and sit down at the next table to Tepas, van Brugge, and the other Dutch pilots.

"You are Dutchmen?"

"Yes."

"Pilots of the London line?"

"You seem to know."

"I've a brother in England now. Could you take him a letter for me? It would get there quicker——"

"If you post it," said Cornelis van Brugge, "it will get there just as quick."

"But the censors hold everything up."

"Sorry, we can't take letters. That's a longstanding rule."

They would get up and walk out into the brightly lit Avenida da Liberdade and mix with the crowd.

"How can you possibly tell?"

"How can you, Quirinus?"

"We post letters here. The British know it. They trust us, Cornelis. But you can't tell about others. Let's go in here."

"*Hola, hola,* two *portos!*"

"What will Hitler do next, Cornelis?"

They watched the crowds bustling through the narrow streets of the old Moorish quarter, the serpentine reflections of fights in the

Tagus, the beach boats close inshore. Behind them an immense row of casks filled the whole length of the wine-vaults.

"I hear they are coming here. Everyone thinks that – right through Spain, and on to Gibraltar."

"Where else can he go – Egypt, Turkey, India, Russia?"

"Do you mind if I sit here? It's so crowded."

They stared at the man, who ordered himself a sherry. He sipped it for a while without speaking. He seemed to be Portuguese.

"You talk Dutch. Are you the Dutch pilots?"

"Yes."

"A friend of mine has just flown over with you."

"We fly lots of people."

"Fine country, Holland."

"You know the Netherlands?"

Tepas and van Brugge glanced at each other. He was small, alert, uneasy.

"Oh, yes, I used to go there on business. For things I can't get any more. You can only get them in England now."

The restless stranger sipped his sherry.

"If I could get my diamonds from England, like those I have in Rotterdam, I'd be well off again. I have a partner there in England. But we can't do business now through this British control. There he is, here I am, and our business at a standstill. That's what war does to us."

"Come on, Cornelis; let's get back to our hotel."

As they walked down the Avenida da Liberdade, van Brugge exclaimed:

"The next place we go to a man will ask me if I don't want to go back to Amsterdam. If you see me make to hit him, hold me back, Quirinus."

"I wonder," said Quirinus Tepas, "if they're after us. Sometimes I think they are. Let's get some sleep, anyway."

They hailed a taxi.

"Grand Hotel, Estoril."

* * *

They chose a steak in the market. The glory of English beefsteaks was no more than a memory, and it was their firm intention to cook it that night in Bristol. They nursed it through the Portuguese Airport control and stowed it tenderly aboard the *Ibis*. It was big enough for a dinner-party. At Whitchurch, with care and connivance, they got it past His Majesty's Customs and Waterguard, down to the Clifton flat, where Tepas, Parmentier, and Verhoeven put it to fry with chopped onions. There was a bottle of Rioja for the occasion. The steak looked fresh after its 1,400-mile flight.

As darkness fell over Bristol, and the steak frizzled, there was a wailing of sirens. And ten minutes later the unmistakable drone of multi-engined aircraft. The Luftwaffe was back. The pilots ran to the windows, watching as the chandelier flares came down, watching as the slow stream of tracer cascaded skywards, then bursts of shellfire near the dim outline of a bomber picked up by the searchlights between clouds. The thud of bombs, the answering thud of guns. The three airmen watched the sky, listening for every change in the pitch of engines overhead.

"That one seems to be in trouble, Theo."

The thud of bombs ceased, the gunfire lessened. At length the sustained note of the all-clear. There was a faint, forgotten odour of steak and onions from the darkened room behind them. They rushed back into the kitchen, where the Lisbon steak had been frying. The air was heavy with the smell of burning. There was a wizened black remainder in the pan. The steak that had come so far was no more.

Their Lisbon manager, Van der Vliet, had taken crew quarters in the city itself, not far from the air terminus. They slept there overnight between flights. It was more convenient and more secure.

The crews, when they wrote to their homes in the Netherlands, gave their wives this new address.

But Theo Verhoeven still used to walk up to the Grand Hotel at Estoril when he had cleared his aircraft for the night.

This pilot was a big, burly man. You could pick him out easily as he walked among the Portuguese. You could have followed him without any trouble at all.

You cannot always see a man following you, but the feeling of being watched is there, if you are being followed. There is a strong urge to turn round.

Estoril was an interesting place even then. The exiled monarchs of Europe were not there yet, but other fugitives of the Hitler war sat about in Estoril. It had many refugees, and in a suite of the Hotel Atlantico was a branch of the German Security Service in Portugal.

"Do you know Estoril well?" the British security officer asked Verhoeven casually one day, as he came on duty.

"Oh, yes."

"Theo, what takes you so regularly up to Estoril, when you are quartered in Lisbon? You're down in the crew quarters now, aren't you?"

"I go up there to collect letters from my wife." "Why don't you get the letters sent to the new address in Lisbon?"

Verhoeven smiled.

"I've been trying to work out what goes on in the minds of the German censor. He opens letters going into the Netherlands from Portugal. If he finds a new forwarding address given, it will be noted systematically and the letters intercepted. When I write home I give no address, and my letters continue to come to the hotel in Estoril. Perhaps in that way I have escaped the notice of the German censors. At any rate, several of the boys who wrote home changing their forwarding addresses have complained to me since that letters haven't arrived."

"Thanks, Theo. You'll excuse the question. We have to ask questions. So you'll keep on going up to Estoril for your mail?"

"Yes, that's it."

"As long as we know."

A year went by and the Lisbon line had carried 1,500 passengers without incident. In the second year it was 4,000, with twice-weekly extensions to Gibraltar. It seemed that the regularity of the flight did not lead either to sabotage or to shadowing by enemy aircraft. Yet the German mechanics at the airport went in to report the British aircraft as they arrived. They ran to telephone the news when the airliners took off for Oporto and London. There could be no secrecy.

"We flew prepared for attack," another long-service pilot, Adriaan Viruly, told me.

The Dutch pilots chose alert-looking passengers and posted them to port and starboard of the cabin to keep lookout at the windows of the aircraft for enemy planes. Rarely did they see aircraft over the bay.

Yet, curiously, when they did see a parallel speck over the Bay of Biscay, the enemy aircraft maintained its distance or turned away.

The Air Ministry calculated that passage of the *Ibis* and its sister aircraft must be known to the German air defences along the Channel coast. Yet 5,500 passengers were flown without incident, without pursuit, without an attempt at interception.

So it came to be said of Admiral Canaris that the Chief of German Military Intelligence had put these airliners under his protection for mysterious reasons: because they were a keyhole into England, and a source of information coming out. For the sake of British newspapers and diplomatic mail. For the sake, maybe, of passing in an agent or getting an agent out of Britain, five hundred flights without incident; only the ever-changing bay, the variable wind, the changeless coasts – and the fields of cloud: snowy valleys and pinnacles, never twice the same. Even when the sky was cruelly clear, no aircraft ever approached close to them. It was as if they were specially protected, and the reason may be apparent if we study some of the passengers who flew to and from Lisbon.

Chapter 8

The Spy-Line

The Germans set up an espionage branch in their Lisbon Embassy, using the newspapers that were flown in daily from Bristol. They planned to infiltrate spies into England on the Lisbon line. They succeeded in doing so. At least the spies reached their destination, though it could never be quite certain that they passed unnoticed.

"Did you see the security guard was doubled today?" Tepas sometimes remarked on this to van Brugge as they left the aircraft at Whitchurch and walked over to the crew quarters. They did not bother their heads further about it – for that was the concern of the British – except to say:

"Perhaps today we had another little spy on board."

Then they would settle down to a game of five-coin spoof in the mess, waiting for the bus to take them in to Bristol.

I have heard of several cases in which spies used the Lisbon line. Sometimes it was Allied spies who had escaped over the Pyrenees, sometimes it was Vichy Frenchmen posing as de Gaullists who came out to London. Then it could be de Gaullists slipping back into France via Lisbon and pretending to be Vichy Frenchmen. There were neutral businessmen who had been cleared by the British Embassy, and there were Portuguese and Spanish diplomats who might be serviceable to one side or the other, but would not risk their status very far for either side, for the rewards were not great and the hazards numerous. Such a case occurred when the German service attachés in Madrid found a Spaniard, a junior diplomat, whom they thought they could use in the sabotage line. His career in espionage began in Lisbon early in 1941. The pattern of his mission was something like this:

"If you want to go through with it," said the German service attaché, "you must get us some results on the British Navy. You have diplomatic immunity. You are employed in England. Of course we could send in a refugee. It's not so hard. We've seen numbers of refugees accepted by the British, but the refugees don't come back, and you can come back. We want you to take up some of our contacts in Britain with the Fascist movement there. We have several trusted men. It's plain sailing for you."

The German was cheerful, persuasive, convincing.

"You can fly more or less as you please," he said. "Perhaps you can contrive to bring out the diplomatic bag. Then you could report more often. The British will give you priority to fly to and from London."

"And in London?"

"You will receive telephone calls. You will sometimes meet a man outside a post office. He will discuss with you the tasks that we have allotted to him, and he will report results."

The minor diplomat listened intently, his dark eyes fixed on the German, straining for the meaning of the operation.

"Another man will call at your hotel, carrying this postcard. Take a good look at it. You must give him this package and get a receipt for it. Ask him when he can send you a report from Portsmouth. You will receive a second visit from him. He will report to you on exactly what has happened in Portsmouth. You must memorise that.

"In the meantime, you carry on with your duties. It is possible that you may wish to send out your report in a diplomatic bag. That you can easily do. The risks are small for you. You act as intermediary in

London with our service of practised saboteurs. On no account need you meet the men themselves. There will be a link. The men who meet you do not actually do the work themselves. They just report back on damage to warships."

"I think I can manage that, Colonel."

"Remember that the man who contacts you will know nothing about you. All he knows is the rendezvous, where he gets his money and reports his results. He is trained not to be inquisitive!"

The travel application of the junior diplomat went quickly through the British air priorities board. He had not long to sit about in Lisbon.

"Who was this contact man?" he wondered. "What was in the package? Was this British Fascist reliable?"

The Spaniard clutched his hand baggage as he settled in his seat on board the DC-3. He did not recognise anybody on board, but he started when the cheerful Dutch steward tried to stow his parcels for him. You can sometimes tell a nervous man by the way he hugs his luggage.

The *Ibis* refuelled at Oporto: the last moment when he might change his mind and stay off. After that he had reached the point of no return, of no return until his job was done.

Why could not the Germans have found someone else? Why should he have to run all these risks? Such emotions seized many agents who flew north in the DC-3s.

How calm the Bay of Biscay was today! The sky was clear – too clear. He thought ahead. He could imagine the furtive calls at his hotel and the page saying:

"There is a man in the front hall to see you. Shall we send him up, sir, or will you come down?"

So these men would be active in Portsmouth – damage observation and damage initiation. Most probably they had contacts with the workers. Perhaps they posed as Communists and worked in reality for the Germans.

"I could have stayed off at Oporto," thought the Spaniard, "but I have diplomatic status. Why worry?"

The *Ibis* banked away from the Bristol Channel towards Whitchurch. As she taxied up to the control tower, Tepas looked out at the reception party on the tarmac.

"The security party's doubled again," he murmured to the co-pilot.

"Interesting passengers, perhaps," said van Brugge, as they filed out down the ladder.

But nobody was held up in Customs and nobody was searched, not even the swarthy little Spaniard, clutching his briefcase. He was cleared through the Grand Hotel at Bristol and caught a train for London. He checked in at his hotel. They were expecting him. He had hardly finished unpacking when the telephone rang. An unknown voice said:

"Señor, delighted to know you are here. Can we meet some time? I'd like to hear all about our friends."

"Good! Come to this hotel tomorrow morning at nine o'clock."

Those were the code words for meeting one of the German agents who was to receive a parcel and arrange a meeting for a later date. The parcel was bulky. It contained perhaps British Treasury notes or forged notes. He had carried it in his diplomatic valise all the way from Lisbon.

Those London policemen; who said that they looked so friendly? Each of them – they were everywhere – might know. Each might stop him, if he stepped outside the hotel.

He was glad to sit about in the hotel. He had locked the bundle in his travelling-case and locked the case in the wardrobe.

Next morning shortly before nine o'clock:

"There is a man asking for you, sir. Will you come down or shall we send him up?"

"Send him up, please, to my room."

The man who was shown in wore a navy-blue raincoat. He was short, thickset, blue-eyed. He had close curly hair. He might have been a sailor or a skilled worker. He held a postcard so that the diplomat could see it. He recognised it as the same.

"I have a letter and a parcel for you," said the diplomat.

His mouth felt dry, his heart beat fast. The man stood there impassively as he unlocked the wardrobe and then the case.

"I know; I have come to hear about our friends."

The man from Portsmouth stood there stolidly, as the diplomat held out the parcel. He did not attempt to take the money. He did not even attempt to run for it when three other men came in without knocking and advanced on them both.

They said: "We have come to ask you some questions."

There was no mistaking these men. The neutral diplomat turned pale. He still held the large bundle in his hand. His thoughts did not respond at first.

The man from Portsmouth still stood there. The others stood close to him now and ignored the man from Portsmouth. They were square, bulldoggish men in plain clothes.

"They hang you in England for spying," thought the diplomat. "The Germans in Lisbon said it was so well planned there would be no risk – no risk for whom?"

"What questions …? I have arrived here from Lisbon to join my mission. You have no right to search a diplomat. I arrived in Bristol yesterday by the Lisbon line. I do not know what this man is doing in my room. There has been some mistake! This parcel, I found it in my luggage, and it doesn't belong to me."

Such was the case of the junior diplomat. He had achieved nothing. He may well have fallen into a trap. By a route not known to me, the British counter-espionage sent a cheerful message to his German masters in Lisbon – "really not a very clever operation".

The bungling was not all on the German side. There was the case of the French General who was flown out of Lisbon to plan secret service work in occupied France with a British intelligence branch in London. He reached Whitchurch and was escorted to London, where he spent several weeks in minute preparation. His role was then to return via Spain and operate in France for the British. I have attempted to reconstruct what actually happened thereafter.

A British official was sitting in his Whitehall office and turning over the papers on this same French General. He was cleared for travel via Lisbon to Vichy France. The official looked puzzled first and then suspicious. A Free French security officer had called on him earlier that morning to say that there were reasons to mistrust the General. That, after high confidence and the most secret work had just been entrusted to the General. From some crosschecks made in Portugal it appeared that there were 'discrepancies' in the General's story. It seemed, moreover, that he was in touch with the Abbé in Madrid, and that heightened British suspicions, for the Abbé was known to be working closely with the Germans.

There must be absolute trust between the Secret Service and its agents. The General had not been truthful. From the kind of evasions he had practised it seemed highly likely that the General was an Axis agent. Unfortunate, since he had been put in touch with an important circuit of British agents in France and was now in a position to disrupt it. Some damned fool of an amateur at work in this new intelligence outfit!

It was just possible that the General had been delayed by fog at

Whitchurch or by passenger congestion at Bristol on his outward journey.

"Give me Security, Whitchurch," commanded the official sharply.

It seemed to him a long time before his telephone rang.

"Whitchurch Movements, check with the passenger lists and tell me if General A. has left."

"He has left, sir. I put him on board myself yesterday. He had top priority."

"Then he's in Gibraltar by now. Thank you."

A cipher signal was drafted to the Rock.

"Important to detain A.17 till fresh instructions reach you."

A cipher reply came back from the Rock:

"A.17 left for Madrid this morning."

Worse and worse. From London a much fuller instruction was drafted to a Secret Service attaché in the British Diplomatic Mission in Madrid. It left that officer in no doubt that the French General must be taken back to the Rock forthwith by whatever means lay to hand, and that on no account must he be allowed to pass the Pyrenees.

Let us assume that the British agent in Madrid was a short, irascible man[1] with an expensive complexion, who figures later on in this story. He would sit and snort at the cipher and say to his assistant:

"London have made a mess of it again. They have been using that General we passed back to them, and he is now on his way through to Vichy with knowledge that can explode our circuits."

"Will he call here, sir?"

"Yes, he'll call here, and he'll probably call on the Abbé, too. It will be interesting to see whom he calls on first, the Abbé or me."

For a while he would glare at the ceiling, and then:

"I will arrange a small cocktail party for the General while he is *en passage*. Get me the Quack, and we will fix him a strong Martini."

To the man known as the Quack the British agent gave his instructions in his private flat:

"Quack," said the attaché, "you have to come to a cocktail party at my flat when I say, and you have to fix a strong cocktail for one of my guests. He must sleep till he reaches Gibraltar."

Such operations had occasionally been necessary in Madrid, when agents of doubtful loyalty had seemed to be changing sides. One or two of them, for instance, had seen rather more of the Rock of Gibraltar than was healthy for them to know.

If all went well, the General could be sent back to Britain from the Rock on the Lisbon line. If the cocktail party was at dusk, the General could be driven south all night, and it wouldn't seem extraordinary to drive an inebriated man past the Spanish customs officers at La Linea on to the British side. That happened sometimes when officers went ashore and visited the bodegas of Malaga and Xeres.

And so a small cocktail party was arranged in the agent's flat. It was a Service affair, calculated to strengthen the *Entente Cordiale* and give the Frenchman just that additional stimulation before continuing on his dangerous mission. The General arrived, bright, mobile, and unsuspecting, and responded quickly to blandishments.

"Have a Martini, General?"

"Ah, you British with your strong cocktails!" answered the French General. "They are so harmful to the palate. But just one, my dear fellow."

This naturally heightened the tension, and the British took to their Martinis in an alarming fashion. But the conversation was free and intelligent, and soon the atmosphere was restored. It would be in fact like many a diplomatic gathering for which the public pays; the party grouping themselves in one corner of the room, treading on each other's feet, and talking loudly into each other's faces. At length it was dark enough for the second part of the operation. By leaning over the balcony, the British agent could check that a car was there to remove the sleeper.

"Now have just one more for the road! A very special, *mon général*, which I have fixed myself! We drink to your success beyond the Pyrenees."

He selected the strong Martini from the Quack and held it out to his guest. The General was carefree. He accepted the glass without demur, and the story goes that he drank the entire potion.

The party went on. The General sat down on the sofa. His eyes were bright and slightly glazed, and his flow of conversation stilted. A faint smile, and then a rather greyish look came over his face. He began to breathe heavily. The British agent came over to him and shook him gently by the arm.

"We must drive you back to your hotel, *mon général*."

Then he looked over his shoulder.

"Quack, I don't like the look of this man. What have you put in his cocktail?"

The Quack bent over the General and opened his collar and shirt. His heart had ceased to beat.

"He is dead," said the Quack simply. "Heart. The drug might take him that way if his heart was very bad, and he had drunk a lot."

They stood and stared at the pathetic grey face with all the animation drained out of it. The General looked an entirely different person, small and hunched and very dead. His knowledge could no longer be dangerous.

"How long will he last, Quack?"

"Not twenty-four hours in this weather."

"And he's got your drug inside him. That will make a nice autopsy for the Spaniards if they open him up. We must get him to Gibraltar."

"But suppose the Spaniards show an interest in the body at La Linea."

"Well, we can't bury him in the English cemetery here without an autopsy."

"Perfectly so."

They laid the General out on the cold stone of the balcony to benefit from the sudden coolness of the night air, and they sat up late that night debating what to do next.

It was no use doing more until morning, when perhaps they could get fresh counsel. One of them was standing on the kerb outside the apartment very early next morning, filling his lungs with fresh air, when he noticed a car there with a Gibraltar number. Then he noticed a very reverend clerical-looking gentleman wearing a 'dog collar,' about to step into the car. Evidently a dignitary of the Church on his way south.

"Excuse me, sir," said the intelligence man, eyeing the vestments and the benign appearance, "would you be driving to Gibraltar today?"

"I'm late already," said the cleric. "Yes, why?"

"We have a very sick man upstairs, and we must get him to the military hospital at Gib. Could I travel with him in the back of your brake?"

The clergyman peered over his spectacles.

"I really don't see why not," he answered.

Which answer was more exactly correct than he would ever know.

The body of the General was carried out of the house to the pavement.

"He looks in a bad way," said His Reverence.

"He gets these fits occasionally. He'll probably wake up on the way down, but they've got his particular drug in Gib."

The General didn't wake up between Madrid and La Linea. His head slumped about when the car bumped. The intelligence man treated him tenderly and spoke to him from time to time. They had started early, but it was quite late before they reached La Linea.

"We have a sick man in the back," the clergyman began, but the Spanish customs guards waved the car on when they saw the priest.

The Army doubtless did an autopsy of its own at Gibraltar military hospital just to see what the Quack had put in his strong Martini. Then, to complete the deception and make amends, they buried the General in the military cemetery under the Rock with full military honours and set up over him a neat white metal cross. Where he, a German spy, it seems, still sleeps among the brave.

Such was the story as I heard it years afterwards in Madrid. And the intelligence war went on, and claimed its casualties, and both sides checked the passenger lists on the Lisbon line for names they knew or faces they recognised. Generals, diplomats, even politicians and war leaders might travel this way.

Chapter 9

Interlude at Abinger

A small, emaciated man peered out of the narrow windows of the inn at Abinger Hammer. You would not have taken him for anyone of importance at first glance, unless you noticed the extreme sensitivity of his hands: moreover, the depth from the top of his head to the tip of his pointed beard, the dark shadows that ran from his temples down his cheek, the sardonic lip and inquiring eyes gave him in certain lights the appearance of an unkempt Velasquez. This was the Yugoslav sculptor Oskar Nemon – not yet a famous man, then leading a precarious existence in Chelsea and Oxford, and occasionally passing a quiet weekend at the Abinger Arms in the green Surrey hills.

He was watching the road with an amused look for a phenomenon rare in wartime England: a strikingly beautiful woman who often used to drive past unescorted in an open American roadster at weekends. Why should she be alone at the weekend? But this time she did not drive past: she parked the car and came into the inn, so that he could appraise her more closely. She was perhaps five foot six in height, light-haired, oval of face, with extremely quick, intelligent eyes. His amused look changed to one of professional interest. He spoke to her, learned that her name was Violette Cunnington, and that she was employed in the making of war films. Before long he asked her to sit for a portrait bust.

The story of Oskar Nemon's work in wartime should be told more fully, if we are to understand the coincidences that bring the sculptor into this story.

Before he started modelling the head of Violette, Nemon had been busy on the head of a woman in Oxford. It was a case with a curious sequel. For during the sitting, as he studied the features and probed at the meaning of passing shades of emotion, Oskar Nemon would ask questions. His pallid fingers worked about the red clay, his mind searched the other mind, and gradually he drew the soul out of his subject.

The woman in Oxford was married, and had a son, she told him, by a previous marriage, who was of military age. The boy was away on active service.

"More than half my life," she said, "is bound up with him."

And with that, she closed her eyes and thought. As he modelled, Oskar Nemon did not at first notice it, but when his work was nearly finished, he saw that he had closed her eyes. His fingertips touched the clay eyelids, but some heaviness about them deterred him from tampering further. They seemed to have closed themselves.

"But that is not my wife as I know her," said her husband angrily. "I don't want a bust of her with closed eyes."

"I have tried," the sculptor answered, and his fingers twitched a little as he related it to me – "I have tried to open her eyes, but I have not succeeded."

"I don't feel like buying a work of that kind," said her husband. "It's not a likeness."

"Well, I'll gladly buy it if you don't," said a third man standing behind them in the studio.

So the husband changed his mind and accepted the bust with the closed eyes.[1]

"Not long after that," said Oskar Nemon, "a telegram came for her. It was to tell her that her son had been killed in battle. She must have spoken the truth when she said that the boy had been more than half her life, for she died soon afterwards. Her husband rang me up and said: "I see now why you saw her with her eyes closed.""

And Nemon replied: "Ah, so you have understood!"

* * *

But what of Violette Cunnington? I asked Oskar Nemon years later, when we met in his Chelsea studio, whether he had modelled her too with closed eyes; but he said that he had not. In fact he had been captivated by her vitality and found no shadow on her face. Her eyes were wide open and full of light.

As the bust was nearing completion, she brought a friend to see it. Oskar Nemon recognised the slender, thoughtful features of the man. It was Leslie Howard. They talked about his work, and Leslie said that he would also like to sit for a portrait bust. He was already sitting for a painting in oils by Reginald Eves,[2] and perhaps the bust could be done in the same studio. Nemon worked there on what became the last portrait of Leslie Howard.

That was in the autumn of 1942, after the filming of 'The First of the Few'. On the night of 31 October, Anatole de Grunwald saw Violette in London about one of two other films that were nearing completion. At parting from him she complained of a slight nasal infection.

Some days later Oskar Nemon was working in his Chelsea studio in the early blackout of a November evening when there was a knock on the door. On the threshold stood Leslie Howard, deep grief in his face. He had come to announce a death.

Violette Suzanne Cunnington had died in the London Hospital on 3 November 1942, after a short and sudden illness. It was meningitis with thrombosis complications. There was an obituary notice two days later in *The Times* and she was buried in Mortlake cemetery on the morning of the 5th.

A few old friends from the film world gathered at the funeral. They saw Leslie Howard come suddenly to the graveside, not even in mourning, wearing a brown suit and muffler. But his face showed overwhelming sadness.

"Leslee!" Among the mourners Anatole de Grunwald remembered and seemed to hear once more the familiar rather strident voice reminding Leslie of time and appointments.

Who was this talented woman whose passing moved them all so much as they stood in grey Mortlake cemetery? Her background is unclear, and even her death certificate showed certain discrepancies. She was aged thirty-two when she died and her name was given as Violet, but the informant registering her death and causing her body to be buried did not give either her name or parentage correctly, and both were amended three years later by the Deputy Superintendent Registrar of Deaths.

Leslie Howard became sombre and reflective. Artists are more deeply affected than most by sudden death in their proximity. His daughter, Ruth Leslie, remembered that he considered, but did not change, his will,[3] which left the Hollywood estate to Violette Cunnington, even though it now lapsed to the Howard family again. Its value was estimated at £175,000.

"My father was much upset by Violette's sudden death," she said, "and he did not wish to alter the will."

Thereafter his film associates noticed that he became morose and solitary. He retraced his steps often to the sculptor's studio.

Nemon began to model the head of Leslie, and as he modelled they talked of this perplexing riddle Death, and whether it could really snuff out such vital beings altogether. Leslie mused about survival after death, and recited lines from his beloved 'Hamlet'. He became interested in spiritualism, dabbling in it as he had earlier shown an enthusiasm for medicine and branches of science. The film work went on under the continued stresses of war.

As for the portrait, Oskar Nemon worked on that, talking at length with his subject.

"He seemed to regard it more and more as his own memorial," said Nemon. "And he exclaimed once: 'It looks as if you have made my death mask!'"

The winter of 1942 dragged on; it was a winter of many deaths, the winter of Stalingrad, unwilling to give way to spring. When spring came, it found Leslie exhausted but still working without respite to finish more films.

"I have been seeing a good deal of my doctor lately," he said on 21 April.

He came back again to the studio and showed a continued interest in the sculptor's work. When I called there to reconstruct this essential part of the story, the bust of Howard was gone.[4] At the back of the studio an unfinished motif in clay stood in an alcove – two beings half embracing and half held asunder. The foreground of the studio was taken up and dominated by later and more famous works: the benign grandeur of Winston Churchill, a monumental work for the City of London, heads of Duncan Sandys, and other notables.

The visits of Howard to the studio suddenly ceased because there was soon another urgent call to distract him. It came in March 1943.

"The British Council would be really greatly indebted to you, Mr Howard, if you could make a lecture tour of Portugal and Spain this spring.

"We have the Astronomer Royal[5] going, among others, but Arthur Yencken, the Chargé d'Affaires in Madrid, is tremendously keen that you should go."

To some of his business associates, Leslie appeared unwilling to accept, to others he did not seem to be reluctant. It meant a change of scene and climate after the long winter. He discussed it with Alfred Chenhalls over lunch at the Savoy. They might be able to sell some Leslie Howard productions to the Portuguese and the Spaniards, he said, and so do propaganda in neutral countries.

Chenhalls liked the idea. Leslie Howard demurred at first. It seemed, however, a duty.

These considerations led him in the spring of 1943 to accept the invitation to Lisbon.

It is widely said in the theatrical world of London that he had a strong premonition of death when he accepted it. The journey itself did not seem to perturb him, but, as he remarked to Irene Howard and Anatole de Grunwald, there was some risk in Madrid, where Axis sympathies were strong.

"The Foreign Office have warned me that I have no immunity, and if I get into trouble there, they can do nothing for me."

There was certainly a sense of foreboding. That must have been reflected both in his words and his mien when he went to sit for Oskar Nemon in the Chelsea studio. At this period the work of Nemon seems to have brought him in close touch with death.

About this time Leslie made his last appearance as an actor in England in Clemence Dane's[6] pageant 'Cathedral Steps', presented on the steps of St Paul's in 1942.

A friend of the film world, Veronica Haigh, congratulated him on his make-up and told him how exactly like Nelson he looked.

"He laughed and said that as a matter of fact he had arrived late, having been held up in the traffic, and had had just five minutes in which to throw on his costume, without putting on one touch of greasepaint. He just *became* Nelson!"

Veronica Haigh remembered the scene at St Paul's, "His playing of the part was so wonderful that, as I watched and listened close by, the thought came to me that the actor and the man of action were simply two sides of the same thing, and here the fusion was complete.

"He seemed to have developed the 'Nelson touch' himself in some strange way during the last months of his life."

Chapter 10

How to use Cloud

In November 1942 something disturbing happened to the *Ibis*. It was as if a protecting charm suddenly forsook the aircraft. This scene opens in the second week of November 1942. The British and the Dutch pilots sat together in the mess at Whitchurch, playing six-coin spoof. The Dutch were hard and persistent at this game of bluff. Above the 'three', 'five', 'double or quits' of the players the pilots carried on a wandering conversation.

In the crew-room Dirk Parmentier sat with a frown of thought at his desk, talking to Quirinus Tepas. The Flying Superintendent was talking about the safety factor.

"I've never seen an enemy aircraft come really close," said Tepas. "Sometimes the passengers have spotted them in the distance, sometimes they have been flying in our direction and turned away. It's quite a time since any have been reported."

"But it's an advantage, all the same, to use the overcast. We must do that on this Lisbon run, Quirinus."

"But how, Dirk, when cloud conditions are never the same twice?"

"Do we fly above or below the overcast, or perhaps right in it?" mused Parmentier. "What do you do, Quirinus?"

Dirk Parmentier did not often share his thoughts with others, though he searched for theirs and questioned the experienced Tepas.

"I fly," said Tepas, "under the overcast. It makes good camouflage and I need not be looking up the whole time. Stay below the cloud, Dirk."

They asked Theo Verhoeven.

"Depending on the ceiling," he said, "I fly above."

"What are the chances of attack, would you say?"

"I wonder, Dirk. We carry the diplomatic mail and we carry the prisoner-of-war mail. The Germans want that badly. And then we take the newspapers, and they grab those too in Lisbon."

"But with the range of their fighters increasing?"

"They've always had enough range to attack us on O-nine degrees West. Look at these Focke Wulfs; they fly out from Brittany round the coast of Ireland and back to Norway."

"But that is reconnaissance."

"Not only reconnaissance; the Focke Wulf is armed."

"But it's true that when we've sighted German aircraft they don't close."

"That's so. They've left us alone."

"They must know we fly regularly. If the German air attaché opens *The Times* every morning of the week on the day after publication, if they time us in at the airport, they know all about us. They've known all about us for the past two years."

"Yes, Dirk."

The clouds were low on Sunday 15 November 1942 over the Bay of Biscay. It was seven days after the Allied landings in North Africa, behind the back of Rommel, and in Lisbon there had been some excitement and nervous apprehension that Hitler would strike back by occupying the whole of the Spanish peninsula down to Gibraltar. Between England and North Africa, the American C-47[1] transports shuttled supplies. The huge naval convoys that had lain at Gibraltar now fastened themselves firmly on the coast of French Morocco and Algiers, ironclad limpets behind the back of Rommel.

There was quiet elation that Sunday in Lisbon among the British passengers as Theo Verhoeven watched them board the *Ibis*. So now it seemed that the initiative had really been won back at last, two years and six months after defeat in the West. First Alamein and then this.

There were twelve passengers for England that day. Verhoeven did not remember anything notable about them. Weather conditions at Lisbon were perfect, with blue sky above low overcast that stretched across the whole of the Bay of Biscay. The cloudtop was at 3,000 feet, so the reports said. Allowing for wind speeds, Verhoeven decided to fly at a height of 10,000. He would be constantly 7,000 feet above the cloud, and so he passed over the Bay of Biscay and neared the Channel.

Ibis was only thirty miles south of Point A, turning-point for the Bristol Channel bearing. Verhoeven had put her on to automatic steering and Alsem, his engineer officer, was filling up his engine log, when he heard a loud staccato overtone above the steady sound of the engines. Verhoeven through the dome of the cockpit saw ahead of him tracer bullets shining to either side. At that moment the steering grip slewed round and seemed to lock hard over.

Two of the cabin windows blew out, and Alsem, ruffled by a cold wind, could see a two-engined plane with a single tail-fin passing fast below them in the end of a power-dive. He saw the shark-like glass nose, the black crosses. A Messerschmitt, no?

No time to be afraid!

"Fasten safety-belts!" he shouted, and looked down 7,000 feet at the snowy surface of the overcast. There in the clouds lay safety, but 15,000 feet away at their angle of dive.

Verhoeven saw the monster sweeping up from under the belly of the *Ibis* in front of them. He closed his throttles, released the automatic pilot, and took her away.

The German plane turned to starboard, gaining height ahead for a second attack. Verhoeven went into a steep dive. A moment later the German had completed his turn and was coming down steeply again, guns blazing across the course of the *Ibis*.

Verhoeven swung the *Ibis* to starboard, going straight in the direction from which the German was coming down. On intersecting arcs the two aircraft rushed down towards each other. Alsem saw the black smoke from the German's guns. He swore loudly and dragged out the self-inflating lifeboat.

The effect of Verhoeven's turn towards the enemy was that this time the fire went over high. The moment of intersection was past in a flash.

The German pulled hard out of his dive, but now Messerschmitt and *Ibis* were on opposite courses, going apart at ten miles a minute. Verhoeven saw the Messerschmitt growing smaller behind and above them as they dived on steeply for the cloudfield. Then it grew gradually larger, coming in astern of the port wing.

Verhoeven turned sharply, this time to port, and once more the two aircraft were diving towards each other. They watched for the flash of his next burst, but then all went white around them. The blinding sun, the black circling speck were gone. They were in the quiet bosom of the cloud.

Verhoeven levelled out at 2,000 feet, flying blind on a course that would bring him out close to the Isles of Scilly.

Alsem came back and reported no casualties among the passengers. He had left one passenger in charge of the raft.

L. C. Dik, the wireless officer, was swearing at his radio set. The aerial had been hit.

The *Ibis* seemed to fly normally and responded to the controls in level flight. Only the port aileron did not answer. The aileron wires had been severed.

Verhoeven checked the petrol tanks. They were discharging at the normal rate. He still had 240 gallons. The engines ran without vibration.

Dik flashed Whitchurch, but the connection was bad. Whitchurch reported poor visibility over Bristol.

Cautiously Verhoeven dipped out of the cloud and saw north-east of him the outlines of Trevose Head. He held course up the North Cornwall coast towards Barnstaple Bay and landed at Chivenor. Later that afternoon, in the failing November light, his twelve passengers were fetched to Bristol by another plane.

"Well, Theo, Jerry tried to get you," said Parmentier.

They were together again at Whitchurch, the mechanics busy on *Ibis*, replacing her aileron wires.

"I must commend Alsem and Dik for their cool behaviour," said Verhoeven.

"Have you any theories about this attack?"

Verhoeven shrugged his shoulders. "Theories, yes," he said; "but how can we know? Look what's happening. There is increased enemy air activity. The Germans may be trying to break the Allied air supply lines to North Africa."

"But how did they pick you up?" asked Parmentier. "From radio talk, from the beacons, from radar? Had you been calling us?"

"Only the hourly call."

"What do you think, Theo?"

"Perhaps he was just searching the area," said Verhoeven. "Why intercept us?"

"I like to stay near the cloud," said Tepas. "Under the cloud you're unseen."

"But with the cloud low at 3,000 feet you can't fly under it all the time, if the wind is strong against you."

They sat once more thinking and saying nothing in the crew-room at Whitchurch, their thoughts in the clouds. The crews played spoof with the airport staff.

"There's going to be more cloud and more darkness for the next ten weeks," said Parmentier. "I'll forward your report to Air Min. and suggest reduction of radio traffic."

So one attack had been made, and by one enemy plane only. That did not sound like a planned interception, though the Germans had sometimes mounted night interception with radar against RAF formations on transit to the Middle East. Perhaps the single fighter had failed to identify the passenger markings. Was this a chance encounter?

"I'll be flying a little more myself," said Parmentier. "I've been too tied up with this paperwork."

He went back to his office to draft a report to the Air Ministry.

* * *

The deep Stalingrad winter brought respite to the Atlantic. The U-boats killed fewer ships, and the aircraft of Coastal Command killed fewer U-boats. In darkness and cloud, air activity was less. For weeks at a time the patrols of Coastal Command saw no enemy aircraft. Still the four airliners flew day after day to Lisbon. The firing of a Very light from Whitchurch control tower and the lighting of flares guided them down in low visibility.

The Dutch crews at Bristol were morose at the loss of the Dutch East Indies. They wondered when they would fly again the Jakarta route. Their airline had moved its base to Curacao in the West Indies. And who could tell when the war would end? A bent old man, a former Dutch Cabinet Minister, came down to Whitchurch and flew to Lisbon, ostensibly to rejoin his future Queen in Canada, but secretly intending to travel on to the Netherlands for he felt an old man and wanted to die at home, resigned to the belief that he would not see the end of the war.

Parmentier watched his crews, just as he knew the British watched them, for signs of unrest and lack of self-discipline. Boredom would lead some to drink and dance, and a few to dabble in the black market in a minor way, but provided all was within measure and did not reduce crew efficiency, Parmentier accepted it. He did not drink himself, and some who saw his cold, inquiring eye on themselves resented his commanding manner. If he wasn't at a party, Parmentier knew what crews had been there and with whom. He seemed to know as much about his crews as the British security officers did.

"You were at that party in Clifton last night," he asked Tepas once in a remembered conversation. "Was anyone drinking too much?"

Tepas smiled. "It was quite an orderly show."

"You're sure?"

"Here's Johnson; he was there – ask him."

"Hey, Johnson, was there anyone at that party last night the worse for wear among my crews?"

"It was a friendly show. Nobody had too much."

"One man was just nicely happy – but not drunk – and I don't think he's on duty today, anyway."

"Thank you," said Parmentier, but he still drummed with his fingers on the desk, full of thought. That is how he was – more exacting, more competent than other men, and rarely satisfied.

"I want to fly again this week, Quirinus," he said. "I'll take your aircraft and you do desk duties here."

So he flew the aircraft in turn, to see how the crews were doing and what the strains of duty were. The Air Ministry had revised the beacon signals and radio procedure for the Lisbon route, to give them greater security and less need to ask for bearings.

"Your suggestions for routeing the line farther westwards and making greater use of darkness are 'receiving attention'," said the Air Ministry. It also sent him a list of ten code groups, all of which applied to enemy aircraft. The first of these – F.G.Q. – meant "am being attacked by enemy aircraft".

A new procedure began in April 1943. Sealed envelopes were issued to the crews at Whitchurch before the Lisbon flight. The

British Embassy in Lisbon issued them for the return flight. These contained the beacon schedules for the day; but, with a happy knack, the Dutch radio operators also used the German beacons, and by watching the calendar soon worked out how often each enemy coastal station would change its call sign and wavelength.

By 16 April the Air Ministry was satisfied with the system of issuing beacon schedules at Lisbon. Three days later Parmentier again took the *Ibis* to Lisbon. It was five months after the attack on Verhoeven. Since then none of the airliners had met an enemy plane on the Lisbon route.

Only three passengers flew from Whitchurch that day:[2] the Swiss courier with his diplomatic bags, a priest, and a businessman. It was unusual to have so few. Cornelis van Brugge bustled along putting bundles of newspapers in the passenger space to trim the aircraft. The Swiss courier settled in amidships and put his black Eden hat in the rug-rack. The priest and the businessman sat on the other side of the gangway. The crew of the *Ibis* that day was de Koning, the first officer; van Brugge, the wireless operator; and Sijbrant, the flight engineer.

Parmentier instructed his three passengers on ditching drill and briefed them for air lookout duties.

Weather conditions on the west coast were reported to be bad when the *Ibis* left Whitchurch, and therefore Parmentier decided to make the flight direct, without the usual refuelling stop at Chivenor.

"The weather report at nine a.m. shows a cold front west of the Scillies. There is enough overcast to fly the short route, to Point D, staying at three thousand feet till the cold front is behind us. I am flying on at four thousand feet after that."

As he approached the Bay of Biscay the cloud layer began to shred and break, showing the sea below, whipped and whitened by a light variable wind.

"By dead reckoning," said Parmentier, "we should be about forty-six degrees North by zero-nine degrees West. Give me a fix."

De Koning set his sextant and was crouching to starboard of him, to make a sun reading, when he saw a black speck in his sextant sights. It was an aircraft coming out of the sun.

"Aircraft to starboard," he shouted.

De Koning dropped his sextant, snatched at the elevator control, and overrode the automatic pilot. Then they saw other enemy aircraft on both sides: two to port and four to starboard. Parmentier was a man of great physical strength, and he handled the *Ibis* at that moment as she had never been handled before.

"Keeping our machine in a steep power dive, we saw gun-tracers flashing past from different directions. I told the wireless operator to give the attack signal, and kept the aircraft in a steep dive, increasing manifold pressure and revs per minute. I felt that our aircraft was hit, and I saw pieces flying away from our left wingtip."

The three passengers had been flung from their seats. No time to fasten safety-belts. The Swiss courier found himself on the cabin floor with his black Eden hat rolling in front of him. There was a bullet-hole right through it.

"That's my hat. Bought it in Bond Street. Hole right through it. Oh God! There she goes again."

Parmentier flattened her out brutally fifty feet above the waves with a force that a less sturdy plane might not have borne. Bullets and cannon-shells splashed in the sea. Red and white tracer flashed past the wings in all directions. In the cockpit mirror they saw the six aircraft diving on them one after another. As they dived, Parmentier swung the *Ibis* this way and that out of their aim.

"I saw one aircraft close on our tail, and brought the *Ibis* in a sharp right-hand turn. My first officer saw that we were at the same time being attacked by another aircraft to starboard, and it tried to follow us up while firing at us. It nearly collided with us, and had to pull up steeply to go over our heads, missing us by only a few yards. De Koning, who had seen this aircraft at his side, turned our aircraft to the left."

South-south-east they saw a cloudbank some twenty miles away. Twenty miles, five minutes' flying! The priest lay on the floor, praying loudly. The courier saw his hat still rolling about in front of him as the aircraft rocked.

Cornelis van Brugge flashed out the attack signal in plain, but he noticed that his transmitter was giving no radiation. The power dive had shaken the transmitter connection and the aerial apart. As the *Ibis* bucked and jumped, he tried to push home the lead again.

"Calling GKH. From G-AGBB to GKH. We are being attacked by enemy aircraft. Position forty-six degrees north, zero-nine degrees West."

Now the *Ibis* was heading south-south-east at 230 mph, and astern and above her in line ahead flew the German flight. Expecting the *Ibis* to pancake into the sea at the end of her dive and their attack, they had formed up to watch events. But the airliner was not, it seemed, badly damaged.

"Two of the aircraft circled round us and gave the impression of watching for us to land on the sea, and it looked for a brief moment as if the attack had ceased, but soon more red and other tracers were passing us from all sides."

Sijbrant laid out the safety-raft ready, and then he began to build a wall of defence across the cabin amidships with thick bundles of Britain's national newspapers. Behind it sprawled one businessman, one diplomatic courier holding a battered black hat, and one priest, praying loudly for them all.

"Finally we approached the cloudbank, which seemed rather low," said Parmentier. "As soon as we were near enough I brought the aircraft into a steep climb. I realised that this was a dangerous manoeuvre, but it was our only chance to escape our attackers, who were probably somewhat surprised, and we saw them then, all six flying in one line astern on our starboard. Soon the first one came in again to attack us, followed by the others. We were hit again, but continued climbing, with, of course, a gradually decreasing rate of climb, as our excess of speed was running out."

Below them the Bay, on either side fighters with the black crosses turning away steeply after attack. Inside the cabin, four men crouching behind the early editions. And then, white salvation fluttering all round them. Once more the *Ibis* was into cloud at 3,000 feet.

"Thin, but fortunately ten-tenths," remarked Parmentier grimly.

He changed course to the west and kept on his new course for about fifteen minutes. It gave him time to think.

"Still flying in the clouds, we checked our position by dead reckoning, and we realised that we would have to cross the cloudless space between the forty-sixth and forty-seventh parallels, should we return to England with our damaged machine.

"We did not want to risk another chance of running into our enemies, and therefore we headed for the nearest land and flew course to Cape Villano."

De Koning checked the fuel-tanks. They had switched from the port rear tank to the starboard forward tank twenty minutes before the attack. Both rear tanks were already empty. The petrol gauges showed that the main tanks were undamaged.

At the Grand Spa Hotel, Bristol, half an hour after the attack, an excited BOAC radio watch had picked up and transmitted the signals from the *Ibis*. They appeared in the Signals log in this form:

From AGBB to GKH
"10.35 GMT Attacked by 6 Ju88."

A laconic message from Lisbon was noted below in the log:

From G–AGBB to KLM, J.P.: –
"Send left wing-tip to Lisbon tomorrow."

Ibis touched down at Lisbon airport at 15.57 BST, just six hours and forty-three minutes after leaving Whitchurch. Three limp passengers walked over to the Customs. At once Heinrich, the German mechanic, walked out from the Lufthansa bay and stared at the damaged aircraft. It had not taken the Luftwaffe Command long to alert their spies in Lisbon.

Parmentier, de Koning, van Brugge, and Sijbrant looked at their aircraft recognition cards. They saw now that it could not have been Junkers 88 that attacked them, for the attacking aircraft distinctly had twin tail-planes and square-cut wing-tips. They were most similar to Messerschmitts. Parmentier checked the damage. The rear port fuel-tank was punctured – the tank that happened to be empty. A few holes in the fuselage, port wingtip badly damaged by cannon-shell. Controls and landing gear were untouched.

When the aircraft was cleared and under security guard, Parmentier and his crew changed and drove into Lisbon with their Lisbon manager. Van der Vliet ordered wine, and they sat and watched the Lisbon crowds strolling past on the pavements.

"It seemed quite hopeless," said Parmentier. "I did not think we would ever sit about in Lisbon again."

For once he drank hard; but, as he said, "We can't fly tomorrow, anyway."

He thought, as he drank, of the strict watch he kept on his own crews.

"Frans," he said, "we must stop this daylight flying, or we shall lose all our aircraft and crews."

He passed his barograph reading across the table. It showed a sharp dip in mid-flight and a steep climb. The barograph needle had travelled just six minutes.

"Six minutes – the longest six minutes in my life," said Parmentier.

"I sat on my damn tin hat," said Cornelis van Brugge. "That's where I need protection."

"There was a cloudbank here," said Parmentier, touching the six-minute point on the barograph. "It was a long climb."

Next day Verhoeven arrived in Lisbon with the *Buzzard*, carrying a spare wingtip.

"The Germans are changing their tactics," he said. "I have seen flights of aircraft on patrol below us in the Bay. If there is cloud they seem to fly below it. Perhaps they are on escort duty to shipping. You were flying at four thousand feet when you met them, Dirk."

"I flew at four thousand," said Parmentier. "The cloud was low, as long as there was cloud. I thought it best to keep close to the overcast. But then the cloud ended. You were flying at ten thousand feet last November and yet you were attacked."

"I could dive into the cloud."

"That's right, Theo. Whereas I had to climb. Attack may come at either level, but perhaps it's best to be above the cloud and dive into it."

"Did they recognise you?" asked van Vliet.

"They had plenty of time to do that. They must have known we were an airliner. They must have known we were unarmed. They took not the least precaution for themselves, simply circled overhead between each attack."

Quirinus Tepas landed in Lisbon next, and Parmentier argued it out with him and van Vliet at their table over dinner.

"Quirinus, it's no use your flying under the clouds as cover. The German patrols are staying low now, and if you're below the clouds you're slow in getting into them. Stay above the cloud. Fly higher and dive in."

The cheerful Tepas was downcast. He said to Theo Verhoeven: "That's the second time they've attacked *Ibis*. The *Ibis* is my aircraft. Why should they do that? I think the Germans are after me, Theo. I'm convinced they're after me. They know me. They want to get me."

He did not say what reasons the Germans had to attack the *Ibis*, but after that Theo Verhoeven thought that his friend was 'seeing Germans', and had something on his mind about them. Tepas went about Lisbon with an air of foreboding.

"Ah, Theo, they're after me," he said.

"Why should they be, Quirinus?"

"Why do they twice attack my aircraft and no other? Why the *Ibis?*" But after that attack there was once more complete calm for the airliners on the Lisbon route.

Chapter 11

The Passengers

When the tide of war turns, the nations do not know the moment of ebb and flow. Only a few clever men can see that, but the movements of people, the flotsam of war, sometimes indicate the direction of the waters. And spring 1943 had a decidedly unsettling effect on people. There was once more a distinct movement towards the white cliffs and green headlands of Britain. More passengers than ever before wanted to get on board the Lisbon airliners.

This was the only route for those who were not sponsored for travel in the trans-Atlantic convoys, and first of all there was the problem of getting as far as Lisbon. It was a Cabinet ruling that those who had left the Old World for the New in 1940 must not return during hostilities by the direct route across the Atlantic.

Nearly four years had passed since the wives and children of those who could arrange it, and thought it then a sensible precaution, had sailed from the England of Dunkirk for Canada and the United States. A school of children taken over to America in 1940 by Lady Timothy Eden were becoming restless away from home. These children had grown up in Ontario and Philadelphia homes in all the comfort surrounding youth in the New World. They could only read of the progress of war. Neither danger nor rationing could touch them there; but British families who had parted in 1940 began to realise that the perils of bombing and siege were less than the perils of separation. An English boy who had reached the age of sixteen in America gravely told his host in Philadelphia that he must return home, or he could not be accepted for Eton, and if a fellow could not go to Eton, how could he be a gentleman?

The British consular people in New York were frightfully sticky, he had heard, and they took the dim view that anyone who came abroad in 1940 should stay abroad for the duration. That was hard luck on a chap who had been rushed away at an age when he couldn't say 'no'. But he heard that there was a ship, a Portuguese ship called the *Serpa Pinto*. If you could get passage to Lisbon in the *Serpa Pinto*, then you could fly home from there. It wasn't so far. He fretted about the park, wondering if he could somehow stow away on board. Others were so minded too.

"We hope to leave here soon," wrote Peggy Stonehouse, wife of Reuters' correspondent in Washington, to her brother John Margetts in London.

She did not conceal her impatience as she wrote her diary of wartime Washington, with its gracious hospitality and its swollen diplomatic missions, and nothing really to show that it was the capital of a nation at war. She longed for grimy old London again, battered and comfortless as it was, and for some job of war work to do.

It will be settled in March one way or the other [she wrote]. Kenneth is working like mad to get a passage. He has suggested he be sent as a war correspondent to North Africa or India.

We would like to travel to South Africa together. Ken would leave me to go North and I would join the South African Women's Air Force. If we can't do that we'll go to England and I'll join the WAAFs, and Ken will go from there. It is something to work and plan for.

I really can't stand this life much longer. I feel guilty about being over here, safe and comfortable. If we had known that life in Washington would be so prewar and easy, we would never have come. This is all very vague. I'm sure we won't get going till April at least.

We had a long vivid letter from Dave Brown describing the North African landings and bullets flying over his head. They slept on the beach and were sniped at. He really was in the thick of it and very thrilled. So Ken is now keener than ever.

Ten years later, as we drove in a taxi together through Grosvenor Square, Dave Brown of Reuters recalled how he wrote from North Africa. He remembered the impatience of Peggy Stonehouse, and how it came about that these two booked their passages home.

The *Serpa Pinto* was really a cargo vessel with limited passenger space. She was fully booked for many voyages ahead. And so it was not until the end of May that Kenneth and Peggy Stonehouse arrived at Lisbon. They arrived with Marriall and Shelagh Eden, nieces of the Foreign Secretary, some of Lady Timothy Eden's party bound for home. There were wives on board going to rejoin their husbands. The *Serpa Pinto* always sailed full. Kenneth and Peggy stayed in the Victoria Hotel, waiting for clearance to London by air. Sometimes there was a long time to wait in Lisbon. This voyage brought, among other guests from Canada, Mrs Hutcheon and her two daughters Carola and Petra, on their way to rejoin her husband, a Gunner Colonel, in England.

That spring also had an unsettling effect on Tyrrell Milmay Shervington, general manager of the Shell Company of Portugal. He received a letter from his son Michael, who had just completed his RAF training and had been given his commission as pilot officer. The letter told him that Michael was about to be posted to an operational bomber squadron in England. Shervington felt that this might be the last opportunity to see his son; RAF casualties in the war over Germany were mounting as the bomber effort increased. He thought that it might be possible to get an air passage to London before the boy was posted. He pondered over this at golf in Estoril, and at his desk in the Shell offices of Lisbon. The idea came back to him again and again; it was hard to dismiss it. He would cable to London and see if the Company would agree to a visit home.

I am told that Shervington was in other ways an important man. Besides being a Shell executive, he was Chairman of the British Community Council in Lisbon which co-ordinated and directed the war work of the British in that consular area. The Germans later described him as a senior 'spy'.

To Gordon Thompson Maclean, Inspector General of His Majesty's Consulates, after thirteen years of travelling around British missions abroad, came another and not unwelcome instruction. He was to make a routine tour of inspection that spring of consular posts in the Iberian Peninsula and North Africa.

"The purpose was to deal with problems such as staffing and salary scales; the latter," the Foreign Office said, "required frequent revision, because of steadily rising costs and fluctuating exchange rates."

He had been Consul in Addis Ababa in 1926, and in Madrid in 1930. He knew the Mediterranean coast and its missions well, and he had made more than one of these tours during the war. It would bring him home to England about the end of May, a few months before he was due for retirement and pension.

Such was also the prospect for Francis German Cowlrick, representative of the British engineering firm of Babcock and Wilcox in Spain. After a lifetime of engineering he was due to retire that May. He sat about the British Club in Madrid, turning over a letter from his daughter and wondering whether he would not really prefer to pass the rest of the war in the Spanish sunlight. In the Cork Club over luncheon he argued it this way and that. Spain had everything to offer to a man on retiring, except the sight of moist green hills and the sound of English voices and the chance to potter about and retrace your steps at the end of a lifetime.

Who else was converging at this nodal point on the Tagus?

Her duties as a clerical assistant in the Cuban consular service took Mrs Amelia Falla Paton to Lisbon in April, *en route* for a consular post in Liverpool.

Of few of these nine passengers could it be said that he or she was of obvious interest to the enemy, but the stories of the remaining two are rather different.

Ivan James Sharp was on an important mission to Portugal and Spain, and one which vitally affected the German war effort. He was the wolfram man. The nations were warring fiercely in the diplomatic field for that precious metal, with its hardening effect on steel.

Early in the war both Germany and the Allies found their sources of supply dislocated. First Germany was cut off from Portugal and Spain, until the blitz war of 1940 brought her forward to the Pyrenees. But Europe was then producing only one-tenth of the world's supplies. The main producing areas were Southern China and Burma, and as Germany regained access to her supplies in Europe, the Allies lost theirs in Asia. They sought new stocks wherever they could be found or bought.

The second task before the British Ministry of Economic Warfare was to find out how much wolfram was being exported openly and secretly into Germany from the peninsula, and that prompted the mining experts of the United Kingdom Commercial Corporation to send out a man of their own. They chose Ivan Sharp.

I suppose the Germans would have termed him an industrial spy. A small, rather sallow man, with dark tousled hair, the face of the mining engineer, Ivan Sharp, looks at me out of an old photograph with bright, inquiring eyes.

At the beginning of the war he had enlisted for service in a barrage-balloon unit, being beyond the age for more active service. Then his release came. He was to report to the Commercial Corporation and become head of a mines branch working in economic warfare.

"Ivan, we want you to report on wolfram production in Spain and Portugal on the spot," said the Ministry officials.

"The figures we have for Portugal vary, but they suggest that this year Germany will be getting between one thousand, five hundred and two thousand tons from Portugal and about half as much from Spain.

"As you know, in Portugal there has been a rush to the hills to start new workings. Can anyone wonder, with prices of five thousand pounds a ton offered not so long ago?

"Now the Ambassador has got the Portuguese to put controls on, and the export duty has checked the first boom; but we want to know what evidence there is that the Germans are by-passing controls, and what your estimates of present production are. Our commercial people out there will give you every assistance and you can take your time about it. As a consultant you may see things the diplomats can't."

Ivan Sharp flew out to Lisbon early in April. He visited one mining centre after another in Spain and Portugal. He went as far as Barcelona; spent weeks with managements, looked over the machinery, questioned Commercial Attachés and vice consuls. As he moved about the mining districts, he had the impression that he was being followed and watched. He moved deliberately, taking great care of the notes he made. He was in no hurry to report. By taking time he would get to the heart of the problem.

At Lisbon he put his conclusions into a long report, carried it to the Embassy for despatch, and then sat back waiting for his air passage home. The wolfram report reached London safely. It gave the economic warfare men in London much of the information that they needed for the next step, which was to ask Portugal to stop all exports to Germany. Ivan Sharp's work was done. He had proved to himself, and he hoped to his masters in London, that the leakages of wolfram to the enemy were considerable, and that the mine-owners were playing a shrewd and calculating game.

"An admirable report," the Ministry officials commented afterwards to his wife.

Ivan Sharp was satisfied that he had uncovered much, and earned these few days in the sun waiting in Lisbon for his passage home. Home was a quiet suburban avenue in Friern Barnet, north of London, a road of bow windows and tiled elevations, rose gardens and laburnum trees. He had been so intensively into his research on the wolfram question that Sharp may have forgotten what his wife had asked him before he left Friern Barnet.

"I don't care about the passage out, Ivan dear, but coming home do see that you get passage in a seaplane."[1]

For the seaplanes of BOAC took a course much farther west than the DC-3s. Some people maybe would have picked and chosen and pulled wires at that time, fussing like VIPs to get on to the seaplane. Perhaps he did remember her words, as he thought of his homeward booking; but I think of Ivan Sharp as one of those quiet, pre-occupied men of the British middle class who are preyed on by tax collectors; who garden quietly in peacetime; who don't ever expect to get very high in life.

And in the same way, in wartime they work on without questioning much what it is all about, as long as the job is done. Neither in peace nor in war do I see his sort putting in much thought for himself: asking for priority treatment, considering himself important because his mission had been important, or taking things otherwise than as they came, as a matter of course, in the order of things.

Chapter 12

The Jewish Agent

The last of those setting out for Lisbon with whom we are concerned was Wilfrid Israel. He had long been an agent of the British Secret Service, thought the Germans. I found the proof that they thought this in a German Wehrmacht confidential book on Britain issued in 1940, with a chapter on British Jewry and a supplement on British spies. There among them was the pale, sensitive, slightly Mendelssohnian face of Wilfrid Israel, with high forehead, light blue eyes, and hair curling over his ears.

I have no doubt that the British too at times thought of him as their own agent; for when I recently mentioned his name to a civil servant who had worked in the Berlin Consulate before the war and was in the British Consulate in Lisbon during the war,[1] the answer was sharp and significant:

"I am not going to tell you about Wilfrid Israel."

But with time and research, the story of Wilfrid Israel can be told, and perhaps it will show that the Germans, and the British too, were not entirely correct in adding him to the lists of the British Secret Service.

I see him as an individualist, a man who was passionately independent in his outlook; but whose birth and background cast him together with strange companions to do special duties.

Wilfrid Israel was born in 1899 to wealth and influence, with ties in both England and Germany. His father, Berthold, owned the old-fashioned department store of N. Israel in Berlin. His mother was descended from Dr Nathan Adler, Chief Rabbi of Victorian England. His fortune was mainly in Germany, but his friends were in both countries. He lived during the first years of the Nazi regime in a flat in the *Bendlerstrasse*, a few minutes walk from the British consulate in Berlin, and held a British passport.

By the time he was thirty-five, Israel had travelled extensively about the world: to Eastern Europe, Palestine, Russia, India, and Central Asia. As a young man he had seen in Lithuania, Germany, and Poland the beginnings of the new Jewish tragedy in Europe; the segregated communities of Galicia, victims of sudden racial outbreaks; the economic problems of Jewry in the Baltic States, and the organised racial hatred of the Nazis.

As a youth he was still preoccupied with philosophy and reverie. His first love was art and his collection of Assyrian antiquities. He created his own atmosphere about him in Berlin, a world in which philanthropy, poetry, the ethics of Judaism, antiquity, and the Liberal tolerant outlook of the English were intermingled.

By 1930 the calm faces of his ancient reliefs had ceased to satisfy Wilfrid Israel. He was no longer in love with statues. The anxious and haunted look in many eyes had drawn him into the conflict of our times. We find a different Wilfrid Israel in the testimony of his friends. The wandering National Theatre of the Jewish People, the Habima, had visited Berlin, and its dramas stirred something in him that would let him rest no longer.

When the access to power of National Socialism brought crisis after crisis for the Jews of Europe, Wilfrid Israel was in the centre of the torment. He was to the Nazis a marked man, for his Liberal sympathies and his frequent contacts with the British. He was besides a pacifist, and had even banned tin soldiers and toy guns from the family department store. The Berlin shop became a place where stealthy work was done to save Jews from the persecutions of the Gestapo. He worked first with his friend and secretary, Werner Behr, to establish a shop emigration department for those of the two thousand employees who wished to emigrate.

Soon it was not only the employees of N. Israel but other victims of Streicher and Himmler that Wilfrid Israel was succouring. He would walk from his flat to the passport office in the British Consulate[2] just round the corner and plan the escape of refugees, not only out of Germany, but out of concentration camps as well.

"The day of the fanatics will pass," was his calm assessment in 1937. "There are other forces in Germany."

But then came the autumn crisis of 1938 over Czechoslovakia and a State-organised pogrom on 10 November 1938. Business premises, synagogues, houses, and flats belonging to Jews were invaded by squads of SS, who set fire to them, smashed, and looted. A selected mob surged with disciplined ferocity through N. Israel's department store, destroying and plundering the stock. The era of the yellow star, the knock at dawn, the extermination camp had begun.

Relying on the support of the British Consul General[3] and on his British passport, Wilfrid Israel restored order in the shattered premises. Being foreign property, the shop could not be as easily confiscated as others. He saw to it that the Commandant of Oranienburg Concentration Camp could do his Christmas shopping at the store. The bill was never paid, and as long as Wilfrid Israel kept that bill, he held the Commandant in his power; for it was a moral offence for a Nazi to shop in a Jewish store, and a matter for suspicion if he did not pay his bill.

Wilfrid Israel slipped into the homes of British officials by night to arrange for the safe passage of people who had been released from Oranienburg.

Sir Michael Bruce, a soldier of fortune, did daring work in Germany and Austria at that time, a Scarlet Pimpernel working for British Jewry. He saw and remembered Wilfrid Israel in Berlin after the November pogroms. Sir Michael met him with the Chief Rabbi of Berlin.

"I do not leave until all my people here are safe," said the Chief Rabbi.

"And I will stay," said Wilfrid Israel quietly, "as long as the Chief Rabbi stays."

"I never heard what became of Wilfrid Israel," wrote Sir Michael in his autobiography; but for a time they worked near each other, secretly planning rescue and escape from the Gestapo, meeting briefly in the street or passing lists of escapees from one car to another at a rendezvous of a few seconds.

What became of Israel? The department store, which had existed since the year of Waterloo, was wound up finally in April 1939, when the war-clouds were piling up in Europe. Wilfrid had the family belongings crated up, packed his beloved antique statuary, and left Germany for good.

I find his traces next in London in the days of the blitz in a civil defence squad, walking round with a torch and a tin hat, checking blackouts, heaving at rubble with cheery, grimy Cockneys. The thought was still with him of the tens of thousands whom the war-lord still held at his mercy. No unpaid bill could redeem them now, in the clash of nations, and yet it was worth trying everything and anything, he thought, particularly for the children.

Wilfrid Israel managed to visit Palestine in the spring of 1940 to see the home at Eretz which the Kibbuz Hasorea movement had started for young Jewish settlers. He had often doubted whether his versatile race could ever confine its genius to the little land of its origin, hemmed in by the hostile Arab states.

This visit, however, and the culminating miseries of Jewry in Europe seemed to change his mind.

"I know that my path is laid down by necessity," he wrote. "I know that the security of Hasorea gives me a feeling of being at home. I go out again with renewed strength, and whatever the future may hold in store, my stay within the country will greatly soften in my heart all that may come, however painful it may be."

So Wilfrid Israel went to Oxford in November 1941 to inquire whether his knowledge and experience could be put to use in the Foreign Research Department of the British Government.

"At the first meeting we were much impressed by the distinction of his personality and the diffidence with which he offered his services," wrote one of the British officials, Harold Beeley.[4] "We recommended his appointment as a consultant to the German and Jewish sections of the Research Department. He was to spend two days a week in Oxford, besides giving much of his time in London to assembling material and considering the questions we put before him."

Thus it was that Wilfrid Israel was able to continue to work for his ideas and his people. As if to free him from the ties of worldly possessions, a German bomb in the night blitz destroyed his London flat and most of the personal belongings that he had saved from Berlin.

In his capacity of adviser on Jewish affairs, he began to propound to his British colleagues the idea of moving the victims of Nazism from Europe to Palestine. He pleaded particularly that the children should be selected, as being less broken and more able to take root in new surroundings. He had seen Jerusalem three times, but would the children ever see Jerusalem if they were left in Europe? When the knock of the Gestapo came for the parents, often the children had been left behind. Some of these waifs had hidden with remnants of the Jewish community in the occupied countries, but many stole away and joined the stream of refugees going south, or joined the resistance. The French *maquis* helped them towards the Pyrenees. Spanish agents could smuggle them across the frontier and more children could be saved if the venture was properly organised. But only assigned residences and internment camps in Spain and Portugal awaited them as yet. That was better by far than the macabre camps with smoking chimneys that Heydrich had built in Poland for the collecting of Jews. It was still no solution for the future. So argued Wilfrid Israel. Why the hazardous escape by night across the Spanish goat-paths if nothing but other camps lay beyond?

It was not easy to convince the British, for every movement of refugees into Palestine had repercussions in Arab states, allies of Britain; but the Jewish Agency in London pressed for a settlement scheme. It sent its elders to meet the Refugee Division of the Foreign Office. The Foreign Office went into the question of immigration certificates with the Colonial Office. They discussed suitability and organisation and numbers, and how the selection was to be made.

So it came about that Wilfrid Israel was released from his work in the Foreign Research Department in Oxford, and went to London to carry out a new task. At Oxford college meals they missed his serene manners and his curious stories about the troubled Europe that he knew so well.

An ardour for his work had seized him: the sense that, however difficult and perhaps dangerous, it was completely right. The Quakers and the American Jewish Joint Distribution Committee would help him. He had hopes that the Spaniards would cooperate. On the threshold of this adventure he wrote to his mother a letter which I discovered ten years later printed in a memorial booklet by his friend Werner Behr.

It is truly such a joyous feeling of real compensation, looking back on the trying times of the past to realise that you could cast anchor in surroundings which once again make life seem to you sometimes possibly even a blessed thing ...

The author, Ian Colvin, in the uniform of a Royal Marines officer, shortly after joining the Corps of Royal Marines in 1942.

An early Douglas DC-3 in flight. The aircraft became known as the Dakota from its original acronym in RAF service: DACoTA (Douglas Aircraft Company Transport Aircraft).

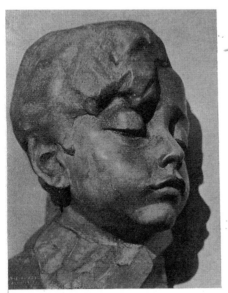

Child's Head

OSCAR NEMON: Born at Osiek in Slavonia (Yugoslavia), 1906. After leaving school lived mainly in Belgium and France, where he has left works in Museums, Galleries and Private Collections. Since 1939 has lived and worked in Great Britain.

SCULPTURES

1.	His Majesty King Peter II
2.	Mr Milan Grol
3.	Sigmund Freud
4.	Leslie Howard
5.	Mr Vetcheslav Vilder
6.	Mr Radoyé Knezhevitch
7.	Her Majesty Queen Marie
8.	Lord Charles Spencer Churchill
9.	Captain Leonard Green
10.	Baroness C. de C.
11.	Dr Miha Krek
12.	Mr R. G. D. Laffan
13.	Mrs Jean Guinotte
14.	Miss Sophie Cosyns
15.	Mr T. V. Giurgievitch
16.	Dr O. L.
17.	Miss Irene Johnston
18.	Mr Voislav Vuchkovitch
19.	Falcon

An exhibition catalogue of works by sculptor Oscar Nemon. (Copyright Nemon Estate)

Leslie Howard facing his likeness with, centre, sculptor Oscar Nemon at an exhibition in 1943. (Copyright Nemon Estate)

Sculpture by Oscar Nemon of Violette Cunnington. (Copyright Nemon Estate)

Leslie with Violette in 'Pimpernel Smith'.

A KLM DC-3 crew at Whitchurch. From left to right are Radiomen Gerard Blauw and Cornels van Brugge, co-pilot Jan Stroeve and Captain Evert van Dijk. The DC-3 is believed to be *Zilverreiger*. (By kind permission of Bonneville, Bergen NH/Jan Hagens, Heiloo, *Londen Of Berlijn*.)

Engbertus Rosevink, the flight engineer on Flight 777. (Courtesy Ben Rosevink)

Tijdens het incident op 19 april 1943 zag BWK Harry Sijbrant nog kans om in de hevig heen en weer slingerende machine het pak met de opblaasbare reddingboot bij de deur te leggen.
Foto: Laden van de 'dinghy' aan boord van de *Buizerd* op Whitchurch Airport. In de deuropening werktuigkundige Arend Faro.

Loading a life-raft on to a KLM Douglas DC-3 on 19 April 1943 are Flight Engineers Harry Sijbrant and Arend Faro. (By kind permission of Bonneville, Bergen NH/Jan Hagens, Heiloo, *Londen Of Berlijn*.)

A victorious Luftwaffe aircrew at Meriquac airfield in 1943 with a Junkers Ju88 in the background. From left to right in the foreground are Leutnant Neccssany. Leutnant Albrecht and Sergeant Freidlein. (Courtesy Ben Rosevink)

Ju88 aircrew members relaxing in 1943. They are (left to right) Leutnants Wittmer–Eigenbrot, Hintze, Muller, Schulli and Gutermann. (Courtesy Ben Rosevink)

Leslie Howard arriving for the film première of 'Pygmalion'

Frank Foley, the Berlin Head of MI6, in August 1939 in London. His work for MI6 entailed visiting Lisbon during 1942–43. (Courtesy of Michael Smith)

At a Flying Fortress base in North Africa, 1943, Mr. Churchill and General Doolittle of the U.S. Strategic Air Force, study air reconnaissance pictures.

A MAN OF MANY PARTS

(*Top*) Left to right, Gabriel Pascal, Bernard Shaw, Leslie Howard and Lady Oxford discuss 'Pygmalion'.

(*Left*) The Scarlet Pimpernel in disguise.

Dirk Parmentier, KLM pilot.

(*Below*) The doomed airliner, *Ibis*.

Quirinus Tepas, pilot of the aircraft.

Baron Oswald Hoyningen–Huene, wartime German Minister in Lisbon.

LISBON. The Praca dos Restauradores e Avenida da Liberdade. Neutral Portugal was the focus of diplomatic and Intelligence activity.

Sir Ronald Campbell, British
Ambassador in Lisbon, 1940–45.

Leslie Howard (*left*) as Romeo in 'Romeo and Juliet' (1936) in which he co-starred with Norma Shearer.

(*Below*) As R. J. Mitchell, designer of the Spitfire, in 'The First of the Few'.

Ivan Sharp, the mining engineer, touring Spain and Portugal to report on a vital war metal – Wolfram.

Wilfrid Berthold Israel, real-life "Pimpernel", in the cause of rescuing Jews from Nazi Germany.

Alfred Chenhalls, 'The Man who looked like Churchill'.

Leslie Howard, at a picnic beach near Lisbon the day before he was killed.

Field Marshal Hugo Sperrle, Luftwaffe Chief of Operations.

One of the Luftwaffe units of Group KG 40 which patrolled the Biscay and English Channel areas in 1943, and shot down the *Ibis*.

Flight Engineer Engbertus Rosevink.

Second Officer Captain D. de Koning of the *Ibis*.

Captain Theo Verhoeven.

Leslie Howard poses in happy mood with Conchita Montenegro, international film star, during his tour of Spain and Portugal.

At one of the last cocktail parties in Lisbon, Leslie Howard and Alfred Chenhalls meet Press correspondents.

Sometimes I thought I would not have strength to carry through my plans. I feared I might collapse prematurely. Then again I feared for many a month that I would have to face being carried away to a dismal fate which I would not survive without having fulfilled my duty to you all – and now with great gratitude and relief I know it was not in vain, that long rather ghastly fight and conflict.

By 23 March he was ready for his mission to Spain. That night he walked up to see Werner Behr, who had worked with him from the beginning. He must have thought it a difficult and dangerous assignment, for he took his will with him, and though there was much else to discuss, the provisions of that will kept returning to his mind: "The sculptures, the art collection to be left to the Kibbuz Hasorea foundation in Palestine. A bequest for the Jewish Youth Aliya, and scholarships on an East–West basis."

He said it was his wish that his body should be laid in a place that he had chosen, in the mountain cemetery by the woods above Eretz Israel.

"Must we spend the whole evening on this will?" expostulated Werner Behr, as they sat in the London blackout of 1943. "You talk as if you were going to a grave in Spain. Let's leave it till you're home again."

His voice broke as he repeated to me, twelve years later, the answer of Wilfrid Israel – a presentiment, perhaps, many people have and usually forget when they return safely.

"I've a feeling that I shall not return."

Next day Wilfrid Israel left London for Bristol and flew on to Lisbon, to undertake his secret mission in Spain.

Chapter 13

Outward Bound

For Leslie Howard, everything was made easy. Sir Malcolm Robertson,[1] Anthony Eden,[2] Arthur Yencken,[3] all thought he was just the man to send to the Peninsula in the spring of 1943. He was the sponsored guest of the British Council, and though not covered by diplomatic privilege – "we can't do much for you if you get into trouble" – still an accepted personality, whose activities would be officially permitted.

Not so Alfred Chenhalls. The chartered accountant and business manager of Leslie Howard sat at his desk in his Chancery Lane offices and pondered over a setback. He badly wanted to travel with Leslie. What were his reasons?

Well, they were manifold. First he liked travelling with Leslie; he enjoyed new scenes and meeting people; and he also thought that his star needed someone cast in a more practical mould to accompany him on a journey of this kind. Recently the vague and the eccentric had come out strongly in the character of Leslie. This Don Quixote needed a Sancho Panza. Besides, there were important business deals to be done, if the Spanish and Portuguese Governments could be persuaded to admit some of the wartime films made and distributed by Two Cities and Leslie Howard Productions Ltd.

Thus it was that Alfred Chenhalls walked on to the scene. He was fundamentally a good-humoured man, always laughing and joking. He was popular wherever he went: fond of the company of actors and actresses; the theatrical world amused him. His likeness to Winston Churchill had not at first been so striking, but it had grown as the war went on.

He was taller than Churchill by several inches, and younger, and he did not have the shambling gait or the head set so deeply into the shoulders. But he, too, was a massive man, pink-cheeked, bald on top, with a domed forehead, and a full rubicund face. His taste in clothes seemed to resemble that of his hero and he ordered his suits from Hawkes and Curtis, though Mrs Chenhalls tells me that he did not copy the Churchill mode or ever understudy him. He went to the hatter where Churchill bought his array of hats, and there Alfred Chenhalls chose himself important black Homburgs. A thrombosis in the leg made him shuffle a little and walk a little more slowly than most men of his age.

Chuckling now, Alfred Chenhalls left his office and went to tell Leslie Howard good news. He had arranged a trip to Spain on official business. He walked from Chancery Lane, down the Strand, a man with the similarity of name and the distinguished likeness that might prove the doom of the *Ibis* and her passengers and crew.

They set out for Spain, Leslie Howard and Alfred Chenhalls, with a light suitcase each and no dress clothes. Leslie carried a limp paper edition of 'Hamlet', and sunglasses stuck in his pocket. As far as Bristol they were accompanied by a secretary and one of the ladies of Denham studios, who said goodbye to them in the lounge of the Grand Hotel.

The lounge of the Grand Hotel, Bristol, was the point of departure – and no return. Beyond that none of those accompanying the passengers could go, and the name of the West country airport to which they were driven by bus was a secret. No relatives might ride out in the airport bus, and the girl behind the desk in the Grand Hotel had seen important people left standing in the lounge with bewildered expressions.

Martin Blake[4] of the British Council happened to be there in the lounge of the Grand Hotel on 27 April 1943. He noticed two men who sat near him at dinner with two beautiful women. He fancied that one of those at table was Leslie Howard.

Next morning Blake was sure of it when he boarded the airliner G-AGBB at Whitchurch. There was a tall, rubicund man with Howard. The pilot was a famous man of the Royal Dutch line, Quirinus Tepas, who pointed with a jolly laugh to a bullet-hole in the upholstery of the *Ibis*, and joked about it.

"That's where a German bullet went on one of our flights. It pierced the Swiss courier's hat, too."

The British air attaché in Lisbon, Wing Commander Schreiber, also noticed the bullet marks as he flew back to his post, and joked about them with Tepas.

"That won't happen again," he thought. "It was one chance in a million."

It was a moderately bumpy flight in glaring sunlight. Leslie Howard wore dark glasses most of the time. When he removed them he looked tired, pale, and unwell. To occupy his thoughts in those seven hours over the Channel and the Bay, he had the subject of his forthcoming lecture: 'The Actor's Approach to Hamlet', and he pulled out the pocket edition of 'Hamlet' and began speculatively to look for the passages that he would quote. He looked up and down the narrow grey fuselage, with its bucket seats and piles of mail-bags. Through the small square windows he could see cloud, broken cloud, and the sea moving lazily far below, but occasionally whitened by the breeze. Chenhalls slept soundly and he too tried for a while to doze, but:

> Sir, in my heart there was a kind of fighting,
> That would not let me sleep.

The heat, the glare, the bumpy flight had shaken him so much that after reaching Portela[5] airfield Leslie had to take an injection before

going on to the hotel to discuss his programme. A doctor was called
and warned him of heart trouble. It was all a little more formal than
he had been accustomed to. He would be required to call on the
Ambassador, but Leslie discovered that he had no visiting cards with
him.

"I don't think I've had any for twenty years," he told his host in
Lisbon, George West of the British Council. So the Ambassador
must excuse formalities.

They put up at the Hotel Aviz[6] and were settling in there when a
call came through from Madrid. It was from Arthur Yencken, the
Counsellor of the British Embassy, to ask whether Leslie could get
to Madrid a little earlier and perhaps do his Spanish lectures first.

"The Duke of Alba is giving a ball and badly wants you here."

"I can't do that, Yencken. My programme is fixed for me."

Next morning he sat out in the sunlit forecourt of the hotel and
began to muster his thoughts on 'Hamlet' in a curious piece of
dialogue. He had recovered from his exhaustion. He was buoyant
again, and dictated with hardly a pause an imaginary conversation
between Shakespeare and himself on the tragedy of Hamlet.

Me: You see, Will, times have changed.

Will: Not as much as you might think.

Me: I mean, after all, you did write for the Elizabethan theatre.

Will: I resent that; I wrote for the theatre.

Me: I beg your pardon. But a great many of your allusions are
         contemporary. They would only be understood by your
         Elizabethan audience.

Will: You overrate my audience. Most of the time they didn't
         know what I was talking about.

Me: Even so, a play like Hamlet, though Danish, has a political
         background which is sixteenth-century English.

Will: Are you reproaching me with writing a play about a country of which I know nothing? Too late. Bacon was before you.

Me: Good heavens, no. Frankly, Will, your anachronisms don't worry me at all – or any of your admirers, I venture to say.

Will: Good. They've never worried me, I assure you.

Me: I only mean that much of Hamlet would be a mystery to a modern audience because of contemporary references and conventions with which your audience would be perfectly familiar.

Will: You repeat yourself too much. I understand. What do you propose to do about it?

Me: Well, we have to resort to a certain amount of cutting.

Will: When you get through – will there be much left?

Me: Within reason, Will, within reason. The mysteries of Hamlet are its greatest attraction.

The lectures in Lisbon were a success. Leslie Howard in dark suit and white tie spoke from the stage of the *Politeana Theatre* on 4 May, and the *Teatro National* on 6 May. At first he described the play as a producer, and then with an electrifying effect began to speak as Hamlet. It was remarkable how he could suddenly create the drama around him, without scenery, costume, or supporting cast.

Between the lectures there was a cocktail party given at the Royal British Club, and Leslie signed the visitors' book in which three English Princes had written their names. On 7 May there was a gala showing of 'Pimpernel Smith' with the man himself to present it. He snatched a few hours away from his hosts to go shopping in the bright streets of Lisbon, for such things as neither money nor virtue could then obtain in England. He and Chenhalls between them bought a large parcel of sheerest silk stockings, to be taken home to their families and the stars of Denham Studios. They joked with

George West about the size of the parcel as they carried it to their hotel, and West had reason to remember this incident, as being material to the Howard story.

The week in Lisbon ended. The two weeks in Madrid were to begin. West and a representative from the Embassy, with quite a gathering of the British colony, saw them off on the Lusitania Express. It was good to have shown the flag in the face of so much Nazi *Kultur* put out by Goebbels and Ribbentrop.

They went in high spirits with Alfred Chenhalls holding the package of silk stockings, and Howard, smiling, a little distrait, leaving the management of things to his companion. The blue train rocked at alarming speed over gradients and curves. This was an important train to watch in wartime, for by this route the diamond smugglers from the African coast sought to get their wares into Germany. Agents and contraband men went to and fro, and Customs men and detectives watched for them to board the train at Lisbon.

So the frontier control was stricter than it is today. Questions were asked about the package of stockings, and it was pointed out that the Spanish Customs would ask for duty on them. They were gifts? That did not matter. The duty must be paid. Ah, so Señor Howard was only a visitor in transit and would be returning to England? Nevertheless he must pay duty, if he took those stockings into Spain, unless ...

The Portuguese officials produced the answer. As Howard and Chenhalls would be returning home via Lisbon, let the package be sent to the bonded warehouse at Portela airport, to await them there. That was a sensible suggestion, so they sent the package back to Portugal and travelled on to Madrid without it, wondering what sort of reception awaited them there at the hands of Falangists, German agents, and Spanish police. And as actors and prominent people do in a strange place, they went to rooms reserved for them in the best hotel in town.

Chapter 14

Countess Miranda

There was a flurry in the lounge of the hotel. In the middle of it was Leslie Howard, signing with a faint reluctance the autograph books that admiring women were thrusting at him.

He was wearing a light grey worsted suit, double-breasted, with his sunglasses tucked absentmindedly into the breast pocket, a grey tie with a silver stripe in it, a light pullover with a subdued pattern.

He murmured to a small, white-haired man who was standing beside him and trying to interview him:

"Can't we ever get away from these women?"

At length he shook them off, and the journalist soon went too, leaving him engaged in conversation with one woman who had stayed behind. There he stood, hands easily in his trouser pockets, an expression of rapt attention on his face. With him it was usually difficult to be sure, despite that expression, that his thoughts were not a thousand miles away. On this occasion perhaps the attention was real.

In the far corner of the vast lounge, sitting deep in the crimson velvet armchairs, were two Englishmen, one with a fierce look and a high complexion, who watched them all the time, as they had watched a good many other visitors to Madrid. His companion, Roger, a middle-aged Silenus of a man, looked first at them and then at his Chief.

"You know, I'm not sure I approve," snorted the British agent. "That woman is suspected of being a German spy and Leslie Howard doesn't yet know it."

"Well, tell her to leave!"

"Not so easy, Roger. She works here in the hotel, and we don't own the place."

"Who is she?"

They sat looking across at her, a small, slim figure with dark hair and exquisite features, the nose slightly aquiline. She had poise and intelligence beyond that of a hotel desk clerk, and the conversation seemed to be going well.

"That is the Countess Miranda. I could show you her dossier, but as I know it more or less by heart, let me summarise.

"Miranda is without doubt a remarkable girl. For lack of a better description I would call her a society woman. The kind that would knock about the world, take a small part-time job here and there, but manage to be at the Ambassador's dinner parties too.

"I don't mean that she could slide into one of Slippery Sam's[1] soirées in wartime, because we've got our security going now at last, thank heavens, but in peacetime she'd be into the Embassy if anyone there interested her – a natural talent for finding out about people, their importance, their incomes, their activities. That makes her a good spy in wartime."

"Have a sherry?"

"Thank you, Roger. Let me go on ——

"I expect at this moment she is telling Leslie that she played as an extra with him in 'The Petrified Forest'."

"Did she?"

"Probably not, but she was in Hollywood, you should know, in the early thirties. Miranda was the daughter of a small Argentine farmer, and I think she must have had a pretty hard struggle in those years, not showy enough, too civilised for the American movie world, perhaps rather too subtle to film well. She saw money there in plenty, but managed to get very little herself. As far as I know, she played small extra parts and then she met a Belgian who seemed to offer her security, until this German Count came along, touring America. He wasn't a very rich man, but he represented two good things at once. He had a position in the world and she was genuinely fond of him, and so she married the man.

"How long that marriage lasted, I can't remember now. It may still be on, but it's immaterial to us here. The essential thing is that she became the Countess Miranda, received a German passport, and travelled to Europe, to live in the Count's large, old-fashioned house in Berlin during the last years of peace. You may have met her there yourself, about the night clubs.

"I've said that the Count is unimportant in her story. None of the men she meets has much influence on her. She moves about and does what she likes. She speaks English, French, Spanish, and German equally well. She has an extraordinarily intelligent mind, a gift for using people, a very quiet, possessive way with those who could be useful to her, and a most endearing manner."

He coughed and then went on:

"Suppose I were to get up and cross the floor to her now! Meeting her after years, she would be just the same to me or you as if she had seen us only yesterday. I'm not sure if I can quite convey to you that sort of command she has over people and situations. However!"

And he coughed again.

"I think she has a special liking for the English, though there's less future with them than with Americans. She likes English humour, English manners, and English conversation. That is what makes her rather a dangerous person for any Englishman to meet in wartime."

By then Leslie Howard had moved off to his suite, and the Countess had vanished about her duties in the hotel; but the man who was telling her story sat there and nodded now and then in the direction of the floor where she had been standing, as if she was still there; and he frowned under his bushy eyebrows at the hotel guests who passed along on the broad carpets, as if they were intruding on his story.

"You may have seen her in Berlin before the war, going about with someone from the Embassy mob, dancing at the roof-garden of the Eden Hotel, or having supper at Horchers."

"Is she a Nazi, then?"

"Well, that's a perplexing question, Roger. She may be a German spy, but she may not be a Nazi."

"How do you know she's a spy?"

"Well, let me go on with my story! Damn you, man, you keep on interrupting.

"Is she a Nazi? I can only say that in the thirties in Berlin she used to make jokes about the Nazi leaders – not bitter jokes, because she had no reason to suppose that they'd ever interfere with her own plans for herself. Hers is the usual attitude of the educated people – that the Nazis are an offence against good taste. But she still serves them.

"I don't think she was a spy in nineteen-thirty-eight or 'thirty-nine. The diplomat she went round with then would just be a good escort, a useful contact with the outside world: dinners, dances, and duty frees. There was no need for her to spy. It was only when war broke out that she found that necessary.

"When the war came, there she was, alone in Berlin. The Count had an aristocratic contempt for the Nazis, but he went to the war, as all Germans do, when war is declared. So she loses some of her sense of security. The Labour Front takes her maid away for war work, or for another family with several children. The Countess too must do war work, the officials say, if she wants to keep a maid in the house. So, for the sake of a maid in the house, Countess Miranda becomes a spy.

"Perhaps I'm simplifying – let's say it was for the sake of doing something exciting too, for the sake of meeting people and having a life of her own, and getting out of Germany, and using her intelligence. Berlin isn't the amusing place it was when she first married the Count, and it's going to be less amusing as the war goes on. I'm quite sure of that.

"I recollect that the first espionage assignment of the Countess was to consort with the Spanish diplomats in Berlin. It may be that the German Security Service had reason to watch them and find out if any of them was serving the Allies. That job lasted a few months, and by degrees Countess Miranda got what she wanted – the prospect of going to a neutral country and living out the war there. In official language, it was a secret assignment to Spain.

"So she comes to Madrid and gets her instructions from Hammes or Wichmann in the German Embassy, or whoever is running their damned security outfit, and he places her here in the hotel, because she is a smart girl and looks well, and with her languages can be generally useful, report on the guests, and perhaps – who knows? – find a way to look in their baggage when they're not in the hotel. If anybody asks her questions she can say she is a Pole, which makes her theoretically our gallant Ally, Roger. Can you beat that?"

"But what is her interest in Leslie Howard?"

"Well, I'm told, Roger, they're interested in knowing what he's doing here. They'll never believe he's come all the way to Madrid just to lecture on Hamlet. He's got his manager with him. So they may suppose that there's a film deal in the offing, one that will fill Spanish cinemas with British films. But they may suspect more than that.

"And there's one other thing that worries me," he added. "Howard is here on a prestige visit, representing Britain. There's a chance that she'll start some sort of scandal to compromise him. Awful if the Spanish police burst in and asked him to leave."

"But you can warn him, surely, that she's an Axis spy."

"That's just what I may have to do, if I can be sure it won't upset what I'm working on. Maybe Leslie Howard can actually help us on the case of the Countess Miranda, if he is let into the secret. This woman is no fanatic. She can be influenced. At the moment I have a fair idea of what the Germans are using her for. Better still if I can use her too. Can I be plainer?"

"Couldn't you get the Quack to fix her a White Lady?"

"That's quite enough from you, Roger," growled the British agent. "I do not wish to be reminded about the Quack and his cocktails. I think that somehow the Germans are going to lose this young lady. All in good time."

"You do something about this?"

"I'll take a risk and assign him a quiet role opposite the Countess Miranda.[2] Leslie Howard is a sensible man, and a very sensitive man. I'm not really worried about him. And I think it will come our way in the end."

He clapped his hands for the waiter, paid the bill, and stalked out of the hotel, glaring as he went at a member of the staff near the door, who bowed so damned low to him and was paid a thousand pesetas a month for reporting to the German Embassy on the guests who frequented the hotel.

Chapter 15

The Madrid Episode

He took up the copy of 'Hamlet', lit the reading lamp, opened the windows wide to the night air, and settled down to his subject. Outside in the Avenida, an unmuted blatancy of continental motor-horns, and the impenitent brightness of neon signs.

It was a cheap, paper-covered edition, with a reproduction of Shakespeare's head from the First Folio. It had a short preface, acceptable to those who believe, as Leslie did, that William Shakespeare and nobody else was the author of 'Hamlet, Prince of Denmark'. He took out a pencil and began to mark his lines in the margin.

> The public playhouse for which most of Shakespeare's plays were written was a small and intimate affair … The stage jutted out into the yard so that the actors came forward into the midst of their audience … There was no scenery, and therefore no limit to the number of scenes … a simple property or garment was sufficient … Such simplicity was on the whole an advantage. Moreover since the actor was so close to his audience, the slightest subtlety of voice and gesture was easily appreciated.

Yes, that was it, the nearness of the actor to his audience. Richard Burbage, when he acted for Shakespeare, was an asthmatic, whose voice would have been sometimes a mere whisper.

Moreover, the silences of Hamlet were as important as his most powerful lines. The New York critics had not understood that in 1936 when they preferred the loudness of Gielgud. They did not understand either why Leslie Howard kept Orson Welles *out* of his Broadway production of Hamlet.

He worked on through the scene on the ramparts and came to the first soliloquy:

O, that this too too solid flesh would melt,
Thaw, and resolve itself into a dew!
Or that the Everlasting had not fix'd
His canon 'gainst self-slaughter!

The apparition of the King – he marked Hamlet's second speech:

Remember thee!
Ay, thou poor ghost, while memory holds a seat
In this distracted globe

and then:

There are more things in heaven and earth, Horatio,
Than are dreamt of in your philosophy.

His attention turned to Hamlet's stage-managing of the play that traps his uncle into showing guilt. Then the Player who sheds tears on rehearsing the Fall of Troy:

What's Hecuba to him or he to Hecuba,
That he should weep for her? What would he do,
Had he the motive and the cue for passion
That I have? He would drown the stage in tears.

He marked the lines 'To be or not to be', and then Hamlet drawing his sword behind the kneeling King. The meeting with Fortinbras marching through to Poland seized his imagination. Here was an allusion to the present day!

We go to gain a little patch of ground
That hath in it no profit but the name.

His pencil moved on to the next speech:

> Rightly to be great
> Is not to stir without great argument,
> But greatly to find quarrel in a straw
> When honour's at the stake.

The hesitations of Hamlet, he thought, might be compared with those in the neutral states who must look on and see:

> The imminent death of twenty thousand men,
> That, for a fantasy and trick of fame,
> Go to their graves like beds.

Could he develop the meaning of those lines in Spain? He thought so, and marked them accordingly. There were other passages, but these were the main ones for him, these and the cupping of his hands round poor Yorick's skull. Ah, here were two lines to mark:

> Now get you to my lady's chamber, and tell her, let her paint an inch thick, to this favour she must come.

He glanced at the conversation between Hamlet and Horatio before the duel … 'you would not think how ill all's here about my heart, but it is no matter' … and then his pencil flickered down the last passage to be marked, with Hamlet sizing up his chances of death:

> Not a whit, we defy augury: there's a special providence in the fall of a sparrow. If it be now, 'tis not to come; if it be not to come, it will be now; if it be not now, yet it will come: the readiness is all.

Those passages would suffice, he thought, to illustrate his conception of the Prince of Denmark, those and the silences of the Prince which he thought so important in a world where the actor stood in the midst of his audience. It was late; he laid the book aside with slips of paper in the marked pages, and so I found it ten years later in Walter Starkie's library in Madrid, and read out of it the actor's preoccupation with death.

At some time in the quietness of his room he must have reflected on a fascinating problem. Who was this intelligent woman on the hotel staff with her interesting talk?

"How long do you think the war will last now, Mr Howard?"

"Till Hitlerism is defeated."

"And what about Bolshevism – don't you see some danger there?"

"One thing at a time. The war was started by Hitler, not Stalin."

"But Stalin is the greater menace to the world."

"That is what the Germans think. Have you ever listened to my broadcasts? And tell me, who are you really?"

It is perilous and often a fault in good taste to speculate on the dialogues of the dead. Neville Kearney,[1] when in a subsequent newspaper interview he threw a hectic light on the affair of Countess Miranda, received a stinging rebuke from Howard's friend and solicitor, Burgis. Nevertheless, the evidence points to her as a disturbing element, and we had better face the fact that a spy was placed near him, and try and visualise his reactions.

The actor was at this time in a restless and emotional condition. Overwork, the deaths of friends, the dragging agony of war itself had thoroughly unsettled him. He had come home prepared to fight the enemy "to the last ditch", but confident also that "intelligence wins over brute force". Yet could intelligence command the game? Was it not apparent in 1943 that it must be force plus intelligence, and that perhaps sheer and terrifying force would take charge in the end and leave baffled intelligence searching for peace in the ruins? The sensitivity of the artist goes ahead and pries out these things. The massacres of the First World War darkened the mind of Nijinsky. Artists in the Second World War reacted variously. Some ran away from danger; others, by the same impulse, went adventuring straight to it.

I see Leslie Howard, in the excited atmosphere of Madrid, forewarned that the curiosity of Countess Miranda was more than that of an ordinary fan, more than a fascinating woman would show towards an attractive man. Actors can never resist a role. If she wanted to believe that he was a British agent on a secret mission,[2] then let her be misled! The result might be highly amusing. He might learn something in turn from her conversation.

Obviously the old record would be played again about Germany being the bulwark against Bolshevism, and was it not senseless then to bomb Europe?

Well, perhaps he would have a faintly elusive air of mystery, and wear a worried air if she looked about his suite, as if somewhere he had a Most Secret master plan concealed. Nor would it stop there – nor did it, I think; for when two intelligent minds are brought together, even if they stand on the opposite sides of the last ditch and argue what is in fact a common problem, they may start with light talk and a defensive wall, but rapidly in such cases the emotions go deeper than was intended. And here Hamlet happened upon a strange love scene, halfway between shipwreck and death, which the conflict in his mind may partially explain.

And when the climax comes, it is clear that Miranda will think herself involved in his death. And the Germans in Madrid will give as an excuse for their action something that may have arisen from the interplay in the hotel – "well, anyway, he was doing secret service work".

Next day he rose late and went to Walter Starkie's flat to discuss the arrangements for the lecture and go on with him to the Cork Club luncheon. Starkie lived surrounded by pictures, books, and the memories of a crowded life. In silver-mounted frames Sibelius, King Alfonso of Spain, Pirandello, and the Duke of Alba thronged his table. His bookshelves covered the walls.

Starkie, as head of the British Institute his official host, was large of body and massive of intellect, with a complexion that had been deepened by the sun, and a rare knowledge of wines. He was a scholar of Trinity College, Dublin, Senior Moderator, gold medallist, Member of the Irish Academy of Letters, lecturer in Spanish and Italian literature, a master of the violin, a man who had studied in Florence, Rome, Upsala, travelled the New World and returned to the Old, written books, and directed the Institute since 1940. Successive British Ambassadors leaned on his great knowledge of Spain in writing their reports home. To the Grandees he was an equal, to everybody a friend.

He explained the Howard programme. The lecture on 'An Actor's Approach to Hamlet' would be translated and broadcast. Leslie would also repeat his other lecture 'How to Make a Film'. There was to be an Embassy reception, a luncheon at the Cork Club with the British business community, a talk to British schoolchildren, more meetings with the Spanish film industry, and the climax a flamenco party in the British Institute building, the Palace Conde Stephen de Canonga. That was to take place on 19 May, and everybody in Madrid would be there: the Duke of Alba, the Ambassador, the diplomats, the film world. As Leslie heard the extent of his engagements, he smiled a wry smile.[3]

He looked pale and tired, they thought. He spoke of his health a while in the language of Hamlet, sitting back relaxed in that quiet atmosphere with the books and pictures.

"I confess I'm not sleeping well," he said. "'*Sir, in my heart there was a kind of fighting, that would not let me sleep.*' This play, Walter, is all about sleep and death. '*I could be bounded in a nut shell and count myself a King of infinite space, were it not that I have bad dreams.*'

"Recently, a dear friend of mine died suddenly, in a matter of hours. I always found it hard to believe that a quick, intelligent mind ceases to exist just because the body gives way. Death is more than sleep."

He mused for a while to himself, then said: "No, I'm not sleeping well, though I'm tired out. Since I've been here in Spain – I don't know whether you believe in visitations and survival after death – I've been getting messages. Dreams, if you like it, and always the same dream. Someone with a message for me – who used to remind me of everything in the studio, because I've got a confounded bad memory. In this dream a dead person is trying to tell me something important all the time, and I cannot understand what it is."

He lapsed into reverie. Starkie saw that he would have to act as shepherd to this strange guest.

He drove off with him to the Cork Club luncheon. It was held in the British Club. An enormous cork decorated the centre of the table. A few silver cups were placed round it.

"Francis, I've had them put out your cups," said Walter Starkie to a spare old man who met them, "because if you're going home to England you won't see them for a long time.

"Leslie, this is Francis Cowlrick, who has worked all his life in Spain, and this is my friend Gordon Maclean of the Consular branch. Gordon is on his last tour of inspection, aren't you?

"I think there will be a dozen of us, but there are some late arrivals. Here's Mr Chenhalls.

"Ah, I want you to meet Wilfrid Israel. He has been making a tour of the refugee centres in Spain. I think you will find his impressions most interesting. He has ideas about a national home for the refugees in Palestine."

There were several more to come. They took sherry and olives. At last the Cork Club went to table, but hardly had they settled down when Leslie sprang to his feet.

"We are thirteen at table," he exclaimed.

Walter Starkie grimaced and turned to Cowlrick.

"Francis, jump into a taxi, and see if you can find Padre Brown[4] to make up the numbers."

He thought that it needn't have been pointed out quite so dramatically, but then actors are strange fellows.

Cowlrick found the Padre. The bother subsided.

Leslie Howard settled down to a long and earnest conversation with the man on his right. The pale, intellectual face of Wilfrid Israel interested him, and he drew out of him the story of his wanderings in search of the Jewish people, in Europe, in Asia, and now on the frontier of the Pyrenees.

"This persecution has left many of the older people quite aimless and broken," Israel said. "My hopes are in the young people, but we must get them to Palestine, to Eretz – Israel. It's wrong that they should fester in camps and *domiciles forcées* here, as if they were still in the hands of Hitler."

"But you *are* the Scarlet Pimpernel," said Howard. "I've only played the part."

"I am getting cooperation from the Spaniards," continued Israel. "I believe that General Franco is proving to be the friend of the Jews. It seems that we can work with this dictator.

"What we need now is entry permits for Palestine from the High Commission, and a ship, if it can be spared, to take the young people out there. I have been visiting some of the assigned domiciles and talking to the boys who are learning to till the soil while they wait for passage home.

"It's curious how at length hope comes back, even if it seemed to be quite extinguished."

Old Cowlrick was bubbling over with the joys of retirement.

"It looks," he said, "as if some of us will meet in Lisbon on the way home."

The British Institute was crowded for the lecture on 'An Actor's Approach to Hamlet'. The audience stretched from the very back of the hall to the feet of Leslie Howard. This was indeed a case of the actor being among his audience.

He was dressed in a brown suit, a shirt with a soft collar, a white flannel tie. He sat in an upright chair and began speaking quite quietly, and during the entire lecture did not raise his voice. His great effects were his silences, said Starkie, in which the audience followed his thoughts.

So he unwound the plot of Hamlet, like a storyteller, without much gesture, and the other characters seemed to gather round him.

The climax for them, sitting in neutral Spain, spectators of a warring continent, was in the Act Four soliloquy, when Hamlet thinks of Fortinbras on his way to battle:

> Exposing what is mortal and unsure
> To all that fortune, death and danger dare,
> Even for an eggshell. Rightly to be great
> Is not to stir without great argument,
> But greatly to find quarrel in a straw
> When honour's at the stake. How stand I then,
> That have a father kill'd, a mother stain'd,
> Excitements of my reason and my blood,
> And let all sleep, while, to my shame, I see
> The imminent death of twenty thousand men
> That, for a fantasy and trick of fame,
> Go to their graves like beds ...

The applause swept the crowded hall and was heard by the Spanish Security police posted outside to see who entered and left the British Institute.

The success of this lecture could not be measured by the response in the Spanish Press; for the Germans in counter-propaganda were stronger than the British, and they were able to ensure that a directive to newspapers forbade all mention of 'An Actor's Approach to Hamlet'. Only in the minds of those who actually heard the lecture the strong impression remained.

The programme went on. The bright days, the late Spanish nights went by. There was an embarrassing moment for Starkie in the last days of the visit, when he discovered that the talk to the British schoolchildren had to be cancelled after some waiting. Leslie Howard had vanished for a whole afternoon, without warning, without explanation. For a moment they feared an accident, or that he might even have fallen into the hands of Axis agents.

He came back distrait, charming, and apologised. His memory was at fault he said. The children's talk had entirely slipped his mind.

"I told you I have a confounded bad memory."

It perturbed Walter Starkie to think that Leslie might also forget the flamenco party that was to be given in his honour. A flamenco party can be a very special affair. The men come wearing a carnation buttonhole, the ladies a mantilla shawl, and a flower in their hair. Everybody in Madrid who counted and was not on the Axis side had been invited, noblemen, artists, diplomats.

Starkie took the precaution of inviting Howard and Chenhalls to dinner first, so that he could produce them at the right moment. He uncorked his wines, lit the candles, supervised the cooking. They were six only at table, Howard dreamy, rather silent.

Eleven years later Walter Starkie nodded across at the silver cups left by Cowlrick, and told me the story of the flamenco party.

"This reminds me of the Bridge of San Luis Rey," he said.

"After dinner there was some unforeseen trouble. I discovered that the flamenco dancers that I had hired had not arrived at the Institute. The guests were beginning to come in. I jumped up from table and left my two guests there.

"At the Villa Rossa in the Plaza Santa Ana the gipsies congregate. There, I thought, I could find gipsy dancers and guitarists. I drove down in my car and got together as many as I could find, several dancers and a guitarist. I drove with them up to the Institute.

"The guests were streaming in, the diplomatic corps, the Embassy people. Soon the British Ambassador would be there, the Duke of

Alba, the Turkish Ambassador and other friendly diplomats. It was a near thing."

The young gipsy dancers were ready, husky-throated and tawny-armed. They arranged their shawls lithely for the dance. As the guitarist began they stepped away from the crowd of guests. The castanets picked up the rhythm of the guitar. The skirts quickened it. Their arms wove patterns. A voice echoed the sad *chola*, all distance and space, the voice of a wrinkled old man tapping the measure, with the dance gone from his legs, but not from his blood.

The elder gipsy woman squatted away from the others, staring at Leslie Howard, as he stood there with the ladies all round him.

The British Ambassador came, mobile and dapper, the Duke of Alba arrived in a dinner-jacket with a white carnation. Cameras flashed at the guests.

The principal dancers began to perform. La Quica danced to the guitar of Mariola de Badajoz. Rafael Leon and Gracia da Triana sang their flamenco songs. Leslie listened spellbound; the idea of a new film stirring.

"This Gracia da Triana dances like a column of fire," he whispered to the Duke of Alba.

"The dance in Spain," observed the Duke, "is a ritual, not a pastime."

And Alba, the Grandee, squatted cross-legged on the floor at the feet of the dancer.

"Roger, do you see who has come in?" The man with the bushy eyebrows glared across the crowded room at another guest arriving with a mantilla shawl and a flower in her hair.

It was the Countess Miranda. She threaded her way coolly through to the group near Leslie Howard, and at that moment the cameras flashed again.

The man who had watched her first at the hotel watched her again that evening. She was entirely self-possessed, and seemed to know not a few of those at the party. Walter Starkie saw her, stopped short staring, but said nothing; and soon there was something else to distract his attention.

Long after midnight he noticed the elder gipsy still sitting and staring at Leslie Howard, muttering to herself.

"Won't you sing or dance?" he asked.

She shook her head.

"I do not sing or dance tonight, and I do not need cards to tell his fortune."

She pointed her finger at Leslie Howard.

"What do you mean?"

"There is death in his face."

"What do you mean?"

"I can only see his skull." She lapsed into silence.

Starkie walked away with an angry exclamation. What with the fortuneteller, and the girl from the hotel, and the dancers who came late, this had been an uneasy evening.

There was a sequel to the visit of Countess Miranda. Next day the photographs taken by a picture agency at the flamenco party were whisked round to the German Embassy, and as a matter of course were checked to see what Spaniards were frequenting the suspect British centre. Among the Spaniards and the British, the Germans saw their own agent, quite close to the British propagandist, Leslie Howard. This perturbed them.

It was one thing to spy on the enemy in the hotel, but quite different to be seen openly at the British Institute. She was, after all, the wife of a German officer, and plainly this was a gesture of independence or of defection. A wavering spy is never so dangerous to the enemy as to her own side. Countess Miranda was summoned to the German Embassy. She must have been expecting the summons.

I do not need at this distance in time to attempt to trace the exact network that connected some of the hotel personnel with the German Embassy in Madrid, or to hazard a guess at the interview that followed. The German Ambassador had many informants: Lenz, Stahmer, the Security Service man, Reyenstuber, Rohrscheidt, Nazi Party Chief Thomsen, and Hammes of the Gestapo. To any of these the Countess may have had to account, and perhaps even to the Ambassador himself.

The outcome was that Miranda had to surrender her passport and so remained a hostage to her masters.

That was about the end of the Madrid episode. I resist any more surmise except to suggest that this was not the ordinary affair commonly attributed by the public to film stars. Before the end of his visit, Howard must have known that she was an enemy agent, and that she was apparently ready to quit the Axis cause. I think he would never have overcome his sensitive repugnance for the world in which she still lived. Yet in his effortless way, despite this barrier, he had dislodged an enemy agent.

On 21 May the Lusitania Express stood at Madrid terminus. The goodwill visit was over. Chenhalls was taking home an audit report on the use of certain Embassy funds. They had both outlined a plan of future cooperation with Spanish film companies in the making of films.

Walter Starkie was heartily relieved, for many reasons, to see his guests departing, and reported to Lisbon to that effect.[5] Leslie stood at the window of his Pullman and waved goodbye to the British colony in Madrid. The Spaniards bowed politely to their guests.

The girl from the hotel stood a little apart from the crowd on the platform, half hidden by a pillar.[6] Countess Miranda shed tears as the train pulled out. Doubtless the Germans too saw her on the platform. Doubtless they saw the tears. But they had made quite sure that she, at least, could not make use of the Lisbon line.

The British agent whose appearance, as I have said, was that of Silenus, had occasion to notice that she shed many tears thereafter.

Chapter 16

The Bay of Biscay

The waters of the Bay moved restlessly between the rugged Breton coast and the northernmost province of Spain. The Gulf Stream, uncoiling its fingers towards the mouth of the Gironde, turned south-west again, past Corunna and Cape Finisterre. The Atlantic tides rose over depths of 1,500 fathoms onto a continental shelf at 200 fathoms, stirring the weedy ravines of the Adour estuary, and breaking in rollers on the Côte d'Or. Yet, despite its reputation, nothing reverberated in the Bay during the first years of the war, but its natural storms.

The Bay raged incessantly to itself. The battle was being fought elsewhere, staining the fjords of Norway, the seawalls of the Netherlands, the Channel ports. When an RAF Sunderland cruised down into Biscay late in 1940 it could reconnoitre at will close inshore, though the Germans were in occupation of the whole west coast of France as far as the Spanish frontier at Hendaye. The pilot flew home, slightly surprised at his calm reception over the Bay. War spread to remoter seas, and major battles were fought in the Java straits, in Arctic waters, and off the Malayan coast, but no such engagement took place in the Bay of Biscay. I find that the aces of the German Luftwaffe hardly vouchsafe a word in their memoirs to the Biscay area.

To their amazement, the Germans in 1941 found themselves able to build U-boat pens in the Gironde estuary without interference from bombers. Among other reasons, it seems that the British Foreign Office opposed such air attacks, possibly hoping to retain a zone of calm in the triangle between passive France and neutral Spain.

But at length the minds of the war leaders turned towards Biscay too; as often in history, they selected the same battlefield without knowing it. The Führer in January 1943 dismissed Grand Admiral Raeder, determined to throw the weight of his naval forces into the U-boat war, and chose Grand Admiral Dönitz to succeed him. Their eyes turned towards Biscay.

Winston Churchill had already given special thought to this battlefield in November 1942. His advisers from the Admiralty and the Air Ministry held that the Bay had become the key to all U-boat operations. So it was decided that a new War Cabinet sub-committee should "give the same impulse to anti-U-boat warfare in the Bay of Biscay as had been applied to the Battle of the Atlantic and night anti-aircraft defence".

The British admirals rubbed their hands and proposed air bombardment of the southern Biscay ports, despite the distressed looks of the Foreign Office representative. The Prime Minister thought of special radar search devices, 'centimetric ASV', which U-boats could not detect in approaching aircraft. He dictated a message to Mr Harry Hopkins,[1] asking that President Roosevelt should make such instruments available for long-range patrols of the Bay.

It was also in the mind of Hitler at this time, as far as I have been able to discover, that Churchill, as the implacable driving power of the Allied war effort, should be removed from the battlefield. He mentioned the idea of assassination in extreme secrecy to Field Marshal Keitel, who in turn related it to Admiral Canaris, and the Chief of Intelligence told General Lahousen, his head of sabotage, what Keitel had said. Hitler did not wish this idea to be too widely circulated, since he was obviously vulnerable himself. But the movements of Churchill thereafter came to be followed with increasing interest by the German intelligence. The Germans came near to knowing in advance that the Allied Casablanca conference would take place in January 1943. A woman agent overheard Allied officers discussing it in a Madrid cafe – but took the word 'Casablanca' to be a code name for the White House in Washington.

So the Prime Minister flew undetected to Casablanca to meet President Roosevelt for the Combined Chiefs of Staff conference. They called for unconditional surrender of the Axis Powers. They also put a high priority on the anti-U-boat war. Until that had succeeded, US troops and material could not be brought over in quantities enough to make a landing in Europe feasible.

The Air Marshals of RAF Coastal Command studied the routes of the U-boats across the Bay. They marked out two broad belts running north and south across it. Liberators and Catalinas were to fly an outer patrol to 15° West; Sunderlands, Halifaxes, and Whitleys would fly an inner patrol 120 miles west of longitude 10° West. This made two broad oblong traps across the path of the U-boats.

Into these traps sailed also the blockade runners from the Far East with the cargoes of Malayan rubber for Hitler. Six of them had been disabled on their way home between January and April. Their raw rubber floated on the waves of the Bay, and the French fishing-boats pulled in their trawls and went after these much more profitable bobbing yellow blocks.

The Biscay air and sea offensive began to take effect. In 1942 the U-boats had been sinking more Allied shipping than the Allies could replace, but new Allied shipping figures in 1943 surpassed the U-boat sinkings. And U-boats were being sunk at a steeply rising rate. In February Dönitz lost nineteen; in March, fifteen; in April, sixteen; but in May, when the Allied Chiefs of Staff put their great sweep into operation, with combined surface patrols and air offensives, they sank thirty-seven U-boats – nearly a third of the total force at sea.[2]

The time had come, thought Churchill, to press forward with the invasion of Europe. He flew to Washington to take "most earnest counsel, in order that the favourable position shall not be let slip".

He was absorbed by the memory of an idea that had once nearly destroyed his career: a diversionary attack on the soft underbelly of Europe. The operations in the Dardanelles in 1916 had been wrongly conceived, said some; but he was still convinced that only vacillation had wrecked the master plan then. The Central Power must now be attacked before there was time to recover from collapse in North Africa. Would Eisenhower and President Roosevelt delay so long out of caution that the Germans and Italians would be able to armour the underbelly?

"After a serious crisis of opinions ..." in Washington, "an almost complete agreement was reached about invading Sicily."

But after that? The Prime Minister urged that Italy itself should be quickly invaded. In six meetings with the President on war strategy, they worked out an "overall strategic concept for the prosecution of the war".

The Chiefs of Staff were a little wary at the thought of being hustled on to the Continent by the ardour of Churchill. They merely promised to "plan operations best calculated to eliminate Italy from the war and contain the maximum number of German forces". This was not enough for Churchill. He complained of indecision to the President. It would be deplorable, he said, if the mighty forces gathered in the Mediterranean did no more than small island operations in 1943. At length Roosevelt decided, as a precaution, to send General Marshall, US Chief of Staff, with the Prime Minister to the battle area and settle the matter there with General Eisenhower.

A Boeing flying-boat carried them over the calm, moonlit ocean at 7,000 feet – no sign to be seen of the Battle of the Atlantic. A lightning flash that hit the plane was the only excitement, though on approaching Gibraltar Churchill noted that "everyone's attention was attracted by an unknown aircraft, which we thought at first was taking an interest in us. As it came no closer we concluded that it was a Spaniard, but the crew all seemed quite concerned about it till it disappeared."

I have heard it said that this aircraft was in fact a reconnaissance machine of the mysterious German 'Rowehl' squadron, which were unarmed, and therefore could fly great distances on intelligence sweeps.

The Prime Minister spent eight days in Algiers. He sent for Anthony Eden. He assembled the British Commanders-in-Chief in the Mediterranean. There in the Eisenhower villa they discussed Allied strategy.

The Prime Minister enumerated the Italian divisions, fifty-eight in the field and fourteen static on the coasts. He counted over all the gains from a stride into Italy itself.

"Southern Italy is a glorious campaign. Sardinia a mere convenience ... My heart lay in an invasion of Southern Italy. I could not endure to see a great army standing by, when it might be engaged in striking Italy out of the war. I was willing to take almost desperate steps in order to prevent such a calamity."

Ike[3] listened thoughtfully and deferentially. When he had heard the three senior Commanders – Alexander, Cunningham, and Tedder – his mind was quietly made up. There would be no delaying ... there would be no repetition of the Dardanelles.

The old man, well content, planned a trip to Carthage, to sit and paint and blink in the sun at those immemorial ruins. On that same day, 31 May, as the Prime Minister in Algiers convinced Eisenhower of his purpose, Hitler in the *Wolf's Lair* was discussing his losses in the Biscay war with the despondent Dönitz.

"The U-boat warfare must be carried on, *mein Führer,* even if great successes are no longer possible."

"There can be no talk of slackening off U-boat warfare," cried the Führer. "The Atlantic is my first line of defence in the West."

The minds of the war leaders were in accord about the Bay of Biscay. The battle must go on. The Air Staff of the Prime Minister began planning his return journey. It was known to the Germans that he was in Algiers, it was known that he would be flying home. The flying-boat would call at Gibraltar.

The Germans from their villa in Algeciras across the Bay could see through binoculars and tripod telescopes every aircraft that landed on the Gibraltar airstrip or took off by daylight. So well known was this that the control tower duty officer would sometimes end his Aldis lamp instructions to a departing aircraft with a sarcastic flash in the direction of the German villa. The spy nest was taken into account in the security planning of Churchill's journey home. The flight would be so timed as to make "a wide loop out by night from Gibraltar into the ocean", and pass the Bay of Biscay in darkness.

Nevertheless security is not served only by darkness and distance. In these days a rumour began to revive in the bars of Lisbon, a rumour which first gained circulation after the Casablanca conference and was once again current. It reached the ears of the Baron Hoyningen-Huene, German Ambassador in Lisbon, as he afterwards confirmed to me.

The rumour ran that Winston Churchill would pass through Lisbon and perhaps visit Madeira before flying on to Britain. Was this part of the security plan that was to cover his real route home?

Chapter 17

The End of May

"What, not yet?" said Leslie Howard, when the two film men from the British Embassy met him at Lisbon railway station. "So you haven't had 'The First of the Few' here yet?"

He turned to Alfred Chenhalls. "I was thinking on the way out that we could have shown it at the Estrela Hall Cinema here, just as we did 'Pimpernel Smith'. Why not?"

The same idea had occurred to Anthony Haigh, the cultural attaché at the British Embassy. As their taxi moved off up the steep cobbled streets of Lisbon, already hot and rather airless, with the Tagus shimmering brightly in the sun of a late May morning, they discussed the possibilities of showing 'The First of the Few' to the Portuguese.

The idea was approved, the British Council extended the visit for one week, aiming at showing the film about 28 May, if it could be obtained by then, or perhaps a day or two later, if there were any delays.

A cable was despatched from the British Embassy asking that the Ministry of Information should send the film out in the next plane.

"We have a few days to wait, Alfred. Can't we move out to the coast? It's too damn hot here in town."

George West suggested the Hotel Atlantico at Estoril. It was situated above the sea, its wide, airy balconies opening right onto the Atlantic.

Earlier in the war a German spy had inhabited this hotel and was to be seen rather ostentatiously reading *The Times* every morning in the lounge, but he had been dislodged, and though Axis agents, some of them society women, used to walk into the small bar to the left of the entrance to listen to bar gossip, it was considered that the Atlantico was a suitable place for an important visitor.

This week of delay suited Leslie. He wanted to rest. They drove out along the coastal road, up the palm avenues of Estoril, and installed themselves at the Atlantico.

From the balcony, lying back in a deckchair, he could see the red-and-orange sails of a sardine boat, a gull or two winnowing the breeze, and a steamer, flying the Portuguese flag, that came slowly up the Tagus estuary. This was the *Serpa Pinto*.

She passed by, to lie alongside the old docks and disembark her passengers, Kenneth and Peggy Stonehouse, Marrial Rose and Shelagh Lilian Eden, with a few others who hoped to catch an early plane to England. Some called at the British Embassy to discuss their priorities at the air attaché's office, but mostly it was done by the clerks at the travel office ringing the air attaché's secretary.

The air attaché, Wing Commander Jack Schreiber, did not often concern himself with the daily lists. He was a man of many interests, knowing the peninsula like the palm of his hand. As well as his duties as attaché, he had property in Spain and Portugal, interests in a hotel in Algeciras, and was also engaged in watching the behaviour of that group of Germans, obviously intelligence officers, who were observing the shipping and aircraft movements at Gibraltar from the roof of the house in Algeciras. They were probably unaware how exactly the tall Englishman who called occasionally at the Maria Cristina Hotel was informed about their activities. A necessary operation, this of Schreiber's, seeing the importance of the sea and air traffic from Gibraltar to London.

All went smoothly in Lisbon during his occasional absences. Daily the airport bus took the London passengers from the Lisbon terminal to join the Gibraltar passengers at Portela, the new airport of Lisbon. The three Portuguese clerks – Basto, Brito, and Bonito – checked the passenger lists with the air attaché's office and asked for priorities. There was a long waiting list for London.

Howard and Chenhalls rested in the sun, asked for news of 'The First of the Few', and chatted with George West. Their host had reason to suspect that German agents might still be following their movements, even in a holiday resort like Estoril. There was indeed an incident when Howard spoke rather loudly in the bar about their probable date of departure. His host warned him that he could be overheard.

"What, the Germans keep watch on a film actor like me?" remonstrated Leslie mildly. "What do they think they will get out of it?"

All the same, he may well have been uneasy. They had watched him in Spain, and there was that girl at the hotel who had become a security risk to the Nazis in Madrid. He had something to tell her, proof perhaps of his uneasiness on her behalf. For a renegade agent is often liquidated in wartime.

"If you are going through to Madrid," he said to Neville Kearney of the British Council, who was travelling on a film mission and had seen quite a lot of Leslie Howard, "I'd like you to take a letter for me and deliver it personally to a girl on the staff of the hotel in Madrid."

Kearney demurred. "I should not carry a letter in wartime unless I know its contents," he said.

"All right," said Leslie Howard, and nonchalantly handed him the open letter.

Kearney read it. He tells me there was no hint at all of the time of flight departure. He was having a pleasant holiday in Estoril and was hoping to get home before long. Furthermore, although he did not express direct concern at her predicament in Madrid, Leslie said that he hoped that *she would be able to reach England soon.* So it was not by that route that the Germans became aware of the flight of the *Ibis,* though the letter showed how far Miranda had gone towards changing sides.

On the other hand, a message was sent to Denham Studios giving the approximate date of their return. Proof of that will follow.

The sardine boats beat along the coast, the river cargo-boats spread their bright sails to the west, or lay in the estuary becalmed in the hot haze. He spent a day in the narrow winding streets of old Lisbon, eating at vineleaf-shaded restaurants, and spent one evening in the Casa Portuguesa listening to the *fado* sung to a guitar.

The fado is the song of seafaring people. There is sadness in the voices of these Portuguese, aware as they are of the distances of the sea and the yearning for home. When the *fado* is sung, the singer puts on a black shawl. And so she did then.

The black shawl lay that May evening of 1943 on the shoulders of a famous *fado* singer. In the dimmed lighting bowls of marigolds shone on each table. She raised her head and with full throat sang of love and parting.

They listened to one song after another. A man in a dinner-jacket rose from another table and came over rather unsteadily to ask Leslie to sign his name on his shirt front. At last they left and wandered down the steep cobbled hill from the Casa, past the Royal British Club, past the little square where under a canopy of palm trees the stone effigy of the poet Eca de Queiroz, in a single-breasted lounge suit, leans sheepishly over his double-breasted Muse. They laughed at the statuary, as everyone does who visits Lisbon, and wandered on, past a sailors' bar with an immense row of port casks in its vaults and a hot, fierce steam of cooking, down a long flight of steps, ending in a square where they espied a peacock asleep in the moonlight above them in a wide-spreading, flamboyant tree. It was surely time to go home.

Next day there was a concert at which the Manchester violinist Philip Newman[1] played Bach's intricate Partita No. 2, and Leslie patted his hand as they drove to the concert hall, to help him to overcome stage nerves. This was on 27 May, and there was still no news of 'The First of the Few'.

The following day Leslie sat on his balcony in the Hotel Atlantico, looking out to sea. He was in a mood of indecision, and in that moment the news reached him.

Collett from the film section of the Embassy was shown up to his room. He found Leslie out on the balcony.

"The film is here now. The reels containing 'The First of the Few' arrived by air-freight at Portela, and have been rushed to the Estrela Hall Cinema, but we can't make arrangements to show it and invite the guests before the 31st."

"I've put off flying once already," said Leslie. "If you can guarantee to get me on the plane early next week, then I'll stay on."

"I think we can promise that," said Collett. "I'll get in touch with Schreiber's office."

So it was decided. Leslie Howard, with no need to pack in a hurry, sat on the balcony and wrote another letter to Madrid, this time to Walter Starkie. "I am writing to you a line, sitting by the side of the Atlantic Ocean in comparative peace and quiet and for the first time I am able to collect my thoughts."

The same afternoon, a thousand miles away in the lea of Dundry Beacon, another man was collecting his thoughts. An RAF intelligence officer opened his black official briefcase on Parmentier's desk in the little office at Whitchurch airport.

"I have brought you some intelligence reports about the Bay of Biscay," he said.

He passed them across the desk to Parmentier, who began to read them with an air of slight impatience. He said nothing until he had turned the last page, but made an occasional note on his pad.

"We know some of this already," he said, slapping the report with the flat of his hand, "Seeing that I have been shot at myself. And now you say that the Germans are in a position to intercept us at any time. Let me turn up the letters I've written to your people about this already."

He jumped up and opened the box file. "Look, this is what I wrote in April, when I first thought of suspending the service."

He glanced out of the narrow metal windows, with their green-painted frames, and could see the British and Dutch mechanics with the cowlings off one of the DC-3's engines. They stood and lay on the wings and joked with a girl in overalls on the tarmac.

"Read this, Mr Russell, please. My letter to the Civil Aviation Branch."

> I confirm that I have asked for a conference [he had written after the second attack on the *Ibis*] in order to discuss the possibilities of improvement of the safety of our aircraft on the U.K.-Lisbon line with regard to enemy action.
>
> I thank you very much for your quick response to our request by arranging a preliminary meeting at the Air Ministry on Friday, the 23rd April, and I would suggest the following points for these discussions:
>
> *a.* Are there indications that the enemy is deliberately trying to intercept air traffic between the U.K.-Portugal-Gibraltar, whether carried out by planes marked as military or as civil aircraft?

b. With reference to the recent attack on G–AGBB, and assuming that this was an 'incidental interception' is there any knowledge about the frequency and the extent of enemy patrols in the Bay of Biscay in view of the chance of a repetition of interceptions of this kind?

c. Can we consider the present approved route via Points A and B as a sufficiently safe one for a daily two–way operation in daytime, also on days when no cloud cover is available?

d. Would it, in respect to *(c)*, improve the safety to change the route more westerly, for instance by extending the line Lundy-Point A to 11° longitude, and follow this meridian to a point west of the present Point B? (This would decrease the payload by approximately 100 kgs.)

e. Would it be advisable to fly a part of the route in darkness, and, if so, which part is considered to be the most dangerous for daylight operations?

f. Should it be advisable to fly the Lisbon route partly in darkness, which airports in the U.K. could be made available as regular operation bases or as alternative landing grounds at night?

g. Would it be advisable and possible to fly a daylight service from Whitchurch to Rineanna (Éire) extended from Éire to Portugal the same night, with a daylight arrival in Lisbon and a daylight shuttle service between Lisbon and Gibraltar; return flight from Lisbon to Éire the following night, with a daylight arrival in Éire and proceeding to Whitchurch the same morning?

h. Would the above scheme *(g)* be more desirable than direct flights at night between the U.K. and Portugal v.v from the point of view of the Defence Authorities?

i. How would radio communications and Direction Finding at night compare with daytime on the U.K.-Lisbon route with regard to radio stations and beacons available? Would this involve the navigation being more dependent upon astronomical observations at night?

The above questions could serve as an agenda for the conference together with any other points which will be raised at the preliminary meeting of tomorrow.

"You had a preliminary conference, I think," said the RAF man, following Parmentier's eyes as he still stared out of the window.

"Yes, we did have a conference. Certainly! It discussed the modifications necessary to the aircraft if we go over to night-flying – engine exhaust cowlings, cabin blackout, the fitting of astrodomes. But to do all that, the aircraft would have to be taken out of service, and the regularity of the airline would suffer. The decision, they said, must lie with me, Parmentier, as the Flying Superintendent. I was told to decide when it should be done. But your Air Ministry officials made it clear to me that they hoped I would continue flying for the time being.

"I got agreement that the Air Ministry would organise and prepare, so that if the decision had to be taken later, night-flying could start with minimum interruption. It seemed possible that more suitable aircraft might be available soon, so that we needn't modify those aircraft out there.

"I suppose it was the best meeting we could get. You see, with so much risk and so much loss of life as there is for everyone in a war, I find it difficult to suspend flying altogether. Instead I've been pressing for a second conference on allocation of new aircraft, so that night-flying can start without any interruption at all. We want the service to go on, you know.

"Look, here's a letter from Campbell Orde, the Superintendent of Routes. He says: 'I think that we should prepare for the possibility of an increase in risk of interception at any time.'

"But there's still no second conference. I have been waiting all this month. I've written to van der Vliet in Lisbon for his suggestions on night-flying and to find out if the Portuguese can give us more beacon facilities. His answers are satisfactory. I think we have brought our preparations to such a pitch that night-flying can be started with a relatively short interruption. I saw him in Lisbon yesterday, before I knew that the Air Ministry was sending you with these reports."

The air intelligence reports, Parmentier realised as he studied them, showed no enemy policy decision or direct intent to intercept the Lisbon airliners. It did show new types of enemy aircraft operating in greater numbers over the Bay, and thus making interception much easier.

"Well, the Luftwaffe is deploying the Messerschmitt one, one, oh, Junkers eighty-eight, and Focke Wulf two hundred over Biscay," said the intelligence officer. "The Messerschmitts have a cruising speed of three-hundred miles per hour, a ceiling of twenty-thousand, two cannon and four machineguns, with a fifth in the after-turret. The Junkers have a cruising speed of two hundred and seventy-eight, three cannon and seven machineguns, and both these heavily armed types have about fifteen hundred miles flying range.

"The Focke Wulf seems to have much longer range, but less armament and speed. All three, however, range far beyond longitude zero-nine degrees West, which is the line of flight of your aircraft."

"Our maximum speed is two hundred and forty," said Parmentier. "Just about that. Have a cup of tea."

Parmentier laughed grimly and began to pace about the little room.

"So I have this decision once more. Dislocate the service and fly the whole line in darkness, or use the dark hours for the worst part of the flight. I can't make up my mind now, and I don't suppose you were sent for that purpose. Give me time to think it over."

His visitor nodded to him over the teacup.

"I'll make up my mind, and write to my airline chiefs on Monday, with my recommendations."

"That is the 31st?"

"Yes, Monday the 31st."

He walked over to the window again to stare at the DC-3 aircraft standing outside the Beaufighter hangars, and the mechanics servicing the port engine, and the hump of Dundry Beacon beyond.

Chapter 18

Last Weekend

And so we come to the last weekend. It is necessary to follow events exactly now, and see what clues they give us to the mystery of Flight 777.

"Is it all set for Tuesday, Jack? Are you sure it is all right?"

That is Tyrrell Shervington of Shell on the phone to Jack Schreiber on Saturday morning at the British Embassy to confirm his Priority A for Tuesday, 1 June. His name was there, and the passenger list was made up, but the names on it did not include those of Howard and Chenhalls.

It seems that Leslie was not quite certain about his movements or his departure altogether. There was something erratic about his behaviour. He thought he would go at the beginning of the week – no more precise than that.

He and Chenhalls wandered into the Casino at Estoril on Saturday night and drank a few whiskies with a journalist named Kenneth Stonehouse, on his way to a war correspondent's job. He was booked to fly on Tuesday.

Alfred Chenhalls was flourishing. He had been strolling along the palm avenues of Estoril, taking the whiff of a giant cigar in the evening air.

On the Sunday there was a picnic on the beach at Praia das Maças. The First Secretary of the Embassy and his wife invited a few friends, and they drove through Sintra, past pinewoods and the vineyards of Colares, and there the Atlantic surged towards them as they sat on the dry, white sand and gulls dipped overhead.

Leslie met Tyrrell Shervington at that party, who said he was flying home on Tuesday, and there was a pretty young naval wife, whose first name was Grizel, who thought she was flying home on Tuesday too. "I'm booked, but I may be going to the Ambassador's dinner party instead."

There is hardly a lovelier beach in all Portugal than the Praia das Maças – the beach of the little apples. Beneath its rocky cliffs and shrubs, the fine white sand formed into a tracery of blown patterns like the lines on your palm. Leslie squatted in the sand, the wind fanning his light hair back from the rather pallid, drawn face. He stared at a plate of food, his thoughts miles away. It was a Sunday to remember, one of those pausing days when things discussed are more important than journeys or the cause of journeying.

A little north of the Praia das Maças was a camp near the cliffs where Wilfrid Israel spent that evening walking with the refugee youths from Europe. He was having a hard time with a boy whose parents had been murdered in Germany and who had lost faith in life. Around him stood others carrying hoes and spades, saying that they had been learning to till the soil and would like to go home to Palestine, if he could get them there.

"What a pity I have to leave already," said Wilfrid Israel, looking at their sunburnt faces and dusty shoes. "I'm awfully sorry we cannot chat any longer. I've got to pack and write some letters before I fly to London. We'll write to each other, and meet again next year, I hope, in Eretz Israel."

At some time during that weekend Leslie and Alfred Chenhalls saw Francis Cowlrick and recognised him from the Cork Club luncheon in Madrid.

"Maybe Tuesday," said Leslie vaguely when Cowlrick asked when he was leaving for home, and Cowlrick hurried off to worry the Embassy into getting him onto the Tuesday plane, but what he didn't know then was that neither Howard nor Chenhalls was firmly booked to fly on Flight 777. Perhaps they had relied on the assurance of the

Embassy that their priority would suffice, and perhaps again it was just the hectic way of an actor.

"Are you sure it's all right for tomorrow, Jack?"

Once more it was Shervington on the phone to the air attaché in the Embassy. This was Monday morning.

The air attaché's secretary expected no more calls that day. The list was made up. It was 5 pm, and the last day of the month, with more work than usual. The telephone rang. It was the booking clerks in the Avenida da Liberdade.

"There are two passengers claiming priority – Mister Leslie Howard and Mister Alfred Chenhalls."

"Must they really go tomorrow?" she said. "Why can't they wait until the second of June? The lists are made up."

"They say they must get off tomorrow. They claim priority."

"The Ministry of Information hasn't very high priority."

"But they are insisting."

"Well, I suppose you will have to take off two others. See what you can do!"

"Is that the English College? Can I speak to Father Holmes?[1] Father Holmes, this is bookings. We are very anxious to help Mister Leslie Howard get to England tomorrow. He particularly wants to travel with two friends.[2] Can I possibly hold you over till Wednesday?"

The changes were made, the passenger list was closed and sent up to Portela airport that evening. There I examined a sworn official copy years afterwards and saw that in fact the names of Chenhalls and Howard were the last on the list, and that Leslie had the thirteenth place.

At Portela airport copies of the passenger list were submitted by the airline to the Security Police and the Portuguese Customs Brokers, according to regulations. There is now definite proof that a third copy went to the German Embassy; for after the war a complete set of all British wartime bookings out of Lisbon to England was found by prowling British agents in the desk of the German air attaché when they walked into the empty German Embassy.[3] The Germans had known the name of every passenger who flew.

So it is highly probable that one of the radio transmitters used by the German Intelligence in Lisbon to report shipping and aircraft movements sent a cipher message to Berlin Headquarters naming the more interesting passengers, and there is some evidence that this was the practice. Which names would then be selected?

Wilfrid Israel was known of old to the German counter-espionage. Leslie Howard and possibly also Ivan Sharp were of interest. It is not likely that the name of Chenhalls was included, though its resemblance to that of Churchill has been mentioned, but we know now from captured enemy documents that the Germans described Shervington as the "former Chief of British secret service in Portugal".

What is certain is that during these days, while Churchill plotted strategy in Algiers or painted in Carthage, the rumour ran in Lisbon that he would stop in Portugal on his way home to England and possibly go to Madeira for a short rest there. That rumour, as I have said, ran in January 1943 during the Casablanca Conference. It reached the German Ambassador in Lisbon, Baron Hoyningen-Huene, from his own Foreign Ministry and dismayed the German diplomats, who foresaw late hours and extra work. Now it was put in circulation again. By whom? We shall probably never know. It would be easily spread about by the well-known double agents who met in the bars of Lisbon, but if the rumour originated with those British experts who plan deception of the enemy and worked out the safety factor when Winston Churchill flew in wartime, it is not likely that we shall ever be told the truth. The reported presence of

German long-range nightfighters in the Biscay area, equipped with radar search apparatus, must have caused them some anxiety.

The film 'The First of the Few' was shown on the night of 31 May in the Estrela Cinema. The actor-producer appeared in dark suit and white flannel tie and spoke a few words to the audience. The British and their Portuguese friends watched the story of R. J. Mitchell, and particularly they were to remember that curious death scene, with the seagull flying overhead.

Tavares d'Almeida, propaganda chief of the Portuguese Government gave a last dinner for Leslie Howard, and, so he told me when I called on him in Lisbon in 1955, inadvertently had thirteen to table at the Aviz Hotel.

"I didn't count them," he said, "but I was told it was so afterwards." Thirteen at table in Madrid, thirteen in Lisbon, and thirteen on the passenger list. An unlucky sequence!

While the film was being shown in Lisbon, Parmentier in Whitchurch was making up his mind about the future of daylight flying. I find a document signed with his bold signature and dated 31 May 1943. He was running over the practical considerations of payload and risk, and the availability of new aircraft. How seldom is a decision made upon one consideration only!

"My suggestion is to continue flying the Lisbon line in daytime," he dictated slowly to the stenographer, "in the same way as operated at present, and try to come to an arrangement about the use of Dakota C-47s by us on the Lisbon line, in which case we could immediately start to fly at night. The Air Ministry are now awaiting our decision as to how we are planning the Lisbon line in future."

Astrodomes ... the line must go on ... it had been a marvellous record of regularity so far ... he must get his Flying Dutchman across the bay ...

The Flying Superintendent looked at the weather forecast for 1 June – a strong south-westerly wind was forecast over Biscay, with rough sea and low visibility. There would be plenty of cloud, and the *Ibis* would probably be flying above the overcast.

Neville Kearney turned up in Madrid that evening and went next day to dinner with Walter Starkie. He had been charged with a letter to deliver to a girl in the hotel, but that could wait.

Over dinner he exclaimed to Starkie: "I flew out with one of those Dutch aircraft. There are only four of them, and they keep up this amazing schedule. I wonder if there's not going to be a terrible accident one of these days."

In Lisbon 'The First of the Few' flickered to its culmination. Leslie Howard came across the stage and bowed diffidently to the applause.

Chapter 19

Flight 777

George West met Leslie Howard outside the airline offices in the Avenida da Liberdade at 8.20 am on the morning of 1 June and together they went on to Portela. The press attaché, Michael Stewart, picked up Alfred Chenhalls and drove him to the airport. Chenhalls pulled out his shiny pigskin case, lit a cigar, and puffed away contentedly, beaming out of the window.

Broad avenues led them to Portela airport, which had been opened a year previously. Only the first floor was then in use, and there Customs, airline offices, and police were all huddled together on one level. Big plate-glass windows round the Customs Hall gave open vision, and there was a wide red-tiled veranda next to the restaurant from which it was possible to see the apron, the repair hangars, the runways, and a line of sandy hills and pinewoods beyond.

The *Ibis*, in her warpaint with G–AGBB in large white lettering on her wing surfaces and fuselage, stood thirty yards from the barrier. She was loading freight.[1]

"How extraordinary, Alfred! We all seem to know each other here! There's Wilfrid Israel, whom we met in Madrid. The man I said was the real Pimpernel!"

"Yes, it's just like a gathering of the Cork Club. Mister Maclean of the Foreign Office."

"And Cowlrick."

"You'll perhaps remember, Mister Howard, we met at a lunch at the British Club here in Lisbon. Shervington! I must say I liked your film last night."

"I'm so glad you did."

"Leslie, here's the journalist, Stonehouse, we met in the Casino. There's hardly anyone on this flight we don't seem to know."

"That pretty girl we met at the picnic? She doesn't seem to be flying."

Frans van der Vliet, the Dutch airline manager in Lisbon, took Shervington's briefcase for him and walked with him over to the aircraft, chatting as they went.

"I hope you are not superstitious," he said. "Do you know this aircraft has been twice shot at already, and this is Flight 777."

Shervington laughed heartily.

"Is that really so? Then I shall get out immediately."

"Mind your head, sir," said Rosevink, and the other passengers started forward from the barrier.

Kenneth and Peggy Stonehouse – it had been so unreal in Washington.

"Mind your heads, please."

Francis Cowlrick, bound for the green hills.

"Please mind your head."

The Hutcheons' family going home.

"May I help the little girl, Madam?"

"This way, please, Mrs Paton."

Wilfrid Israel was exhilarated at his success. He had left copies of his lists of young volunteers for Palestine with the Quaker Mission.

"You are Mister Sharp? Mind your head, please."

"Good morning, Mister Maclean."

Alfred Chenhalls threw away his cigar, and, his VIP look accentuated by his slow walk, went across to the aircraft, after shaking hands with George West and the others. The Portuguese smiled and bowed. Quite a crowd there to see them off.

Last of all came Leslie Howard, and he paused on the ladder and suddenly turned back, hurried to the barrier, and beckoned to

George West. It was then 09.25, and the plane was due to take off at 09.30.

"I've forgotten the stockings," exclaimed Leslie.

West snatched the green receipt ticket that he was waving and hurried off to the bonded warehouse, while everything waited.

During embarkation there was absolutely no screen or security barrier. Every passenger could be seen from close range as he passed. The passengers could be counted as they joined the aircraft. Most British and Portuguese personnel were engaged that morning at the BOAC moorings on the Tagus and the seaplane jetty unloading seaplanes, but van der Vliet, who was at Portela, noticed nothing unusual. There is a slight discrepancy in the accounts given to me of seating accommodation. The Dutch company stated that thirteen was the maximum passenger seating. The passenger list showed thirteen names. British personnel in Lisbon remembered that there were extra seats put in according to weight and payload, and that sometimes fifteen and more could fly with the *Ibis*, but it is fairly certain that no British military personnel from the Middle East were added to that flight,[2] as their names, or cover names, would have to be shown on the passenger list. So in fact the *Ibis* left with a crew of four and thirteen passengers, a coincidence which this time may have escaped the notice of Francis Cowlrick.

West thought that he had done well to be back in five minutes. Howard seized his precious package for the ladies of Denham Studios, waved to some Portuguese film executives who had come to see him off, and hurried across the tarmac.

Rosevink, the mechanic, closed the passenger door.[3] Quirinus Tepas moved her slowly towards the runway and took off at 09.35. The *Ibis* left five minutes behind schedule – the five minutes that it had taken to retrieve the package from Customs.

Cornelis van Brugge called Whitchurch Control at 09.40, airborne and leaving Portela airport behind them. His cipher message read:

From AGBB to GKH – Flight 777 left Portela 09.40. Thirteen passengers on board.

Then there was wireless silence till twenty minutes past each hour, when up came the call sign *from AGBB to GKH ...*

Quirinus Tepas took the *Ibis* up towards her ceiling. He would have a strong wind on his port beam. The overcast would be low.

Ibis gave her position at 10.20 BST, again at 11.20, and at 12.20. Theo Verhoeven, as duty pilot at Whitchurch, received van Brugge's messages from the control tower. It was bright in the June sun as they sat unfastening their safety-belts. Rosevink explained the safety drill.

"Now, ladies and gentlemen, you each have a lifejacket under your seat which is slipped over the head and fastened with these tapes at the waist. We carry two rubber dinghies, in case we have to ditch. You will be so good as to report to me any aircraft movements you may see from your windows. We are flying at nearly ten thousand feet, owing to a strong cross wind. Captain Tepas and the crew wish you a comfortable journey."

The familiar glare at that altitude called for sunglasses. They stared at the empty sky and the cloud-floes beneath them. There was not much line of vision upwards, except through a small window in the washroom, but that lay to port, and so on the northward journey only gave vision westwards.

Twenty minutes after the *Ibis* left Portela, Flight Lieutenant Bellstedt of Bremen left the operations room of Luftwaffe Fighter Wing 40 at Kerhouin-Bastard airfield near Lorient and walked over to his aircraft. This wing was attached to the German Western Naval Command for U-boat protection and Biscay patrols.

His *Staffel* stood ready for take-off, low-wing twin-engined fighters with the black cross painted on the fuselage amidships and on the wing surfaces, a swastika on each side of the tail-plane. These were Junkers 88 C6s, mounting three 20-millimetre cannon firing ahead and three 7.9-millimetre machine guns in the nose, as well as two turret-mounted cannon. A formidable armament, able to duel with any bomber that Coastal Command could put over the Bay.

Bellstedt's *Staffel* worked slowly down the Bay, square searching over the same area as was known to Coastal Command as 'Derange'. It moved in chessboard pattern between 09° West and 14° West, sweeping southwards towards Cape Villano.

"Drizzly," remarked Peter Friedlein, radio operator in the sixth plane, as they reached the area of 46° North and 09° West.

The roof of the cloud below them was roughened and windswept, and where the sea was visible, it was whipped white. Not favourable weather for a search, and until 12.45 they had sighted nothing.

But at 12.45 Lieutenant Bellstedt called over the intercom:

"*Achtung*, single aircraft on north-easterly course. Line ahead!"

For nine minutes[4] they crept forward towards the DC-3, flying some 4,000 feet above the cloud. They gained height on her and drew in till her white markings were plainly visible.

Oh, Quirinus, why do you fly so high!

On the ninth minute, at 12.54, Whitchurch control tower received two signals in quick succession.

> *From AGBB to GKH – ... an unidentified aircraft follows me.*
> *From AGBB to GKH – ... am attacked by enemy aircraft.*

Whitchurch Control called back the *Ibis* and went on calling. There was no reply. It could be that the radio had been shot away, or the aerial torn loose. That had happened with van Brugge once before on 19 April, they remembered. They waited for the 1.20 call from the *Ibis*. She called them no more.

From the sixth aircraft Friedlein watched them go in to the kill from the rear and the starboard beam.

Once more the flashing spears of light all round the *Ibis*, once more the steep, steep dive; but the cloud was so far away. This time the tanks were hit and she dived on in flames.

As the last three aircraft veered away to re-form, they saw a dreadful sight. The after-door of the *Ibis* was wrenched open and four men sprang out into the void.[5] A single parachute unfurled, caught fire, and went with increasing speed like a flaming meteor into the cloud.

Ahead of it blazed the *Ibis* for a few seconds yet, till she pierced the overcast; and shortly afterwards the sea also, where her anguish was quenched.

She sank like a stone, and when the Germans dipped warily through the cloud they saw no survivors in the low mist and chopped seas. They formed up, and returned to base.

At Whitchurch they calculated that the fuel of the *Ibis* could last her till 6 pm, but 6 pm came and no report of her.

The telephone rang in the pilot's room. Verhoeven lifted the receiver.

"What time will Cornelis be in?" – his wife was calling up from the house below Dundry Hill.

"No news yet," said Verhoeven. "Let me call you back. Johnson, go over and tell her what has happened."

They calculated that Von Weyrote and Alsem in the *Buzzard* going south that day had passed over the exact spot – within half an hour of the interception taking place. But a message from the British Embassy in Lisbon told them that Von Weyrote had reported an uneventful journey. He had seen nothing.

A party of American soldiers, who had come to Whitchurch from the nearby depot with some cans of pineapple juice and a bottle of gin to welcome Leslie Howard home, dropped the cans back into their duffle pockets and trudged back to their mess. The airline courier drove from Whitchurch to the Grand Hotel in Bristol to see that next of kin were told the aircraft was overdue and feared lost.

There he found the titian-haired girl at the desk in some distress. All day there had been inquiries for the aircraft, and it had been possible to tell those who were next of kin, but there were two ladies in the hotel, she said, who had come several times to the desk and asked for news of the flight. They couldn't be told under security regulations. She thought they were friends of Leslie Howard and his partner, Mr Chenhalls.

The courier walked over to them, and said, "If you have come to meet Flight 777, I am sorry to tell you that the aircraft is overdue and feared lost through enemy action."

Quite considerably later that night both women were still sitting in the lounge of the Grand Hotel. They drank whisky. The hall porter tried to cheer them up while the news spread outside, the way such news will, deepening the blackout of Bristol.

Two days later Leslie Howard's last message reached home at Stowe Maries. It was addressed to his wife, Ruth. It had been delayed by censorship. It said: *Home for dinner.*

Chapter 20

Aftermath

Neville Kearney had arrived in Madrid on 1 June, and spent most of the following day at the British Embassy. As he was leaving he learned from the Information Room that the *Ibis* was missing, and Leslie Howard, with all aboard, feared lost. He walked into the hotel ruminating on the letter in his pocket, went upstairs, and asked for the Countess. He could say nothing, for the information of the loss of the aircraft was confidential, and merely handed her the letter.

She opened it in his presence and read it with evident delight, sitting on a couch and turning the pages over. Then she handed it to him to read, and he glanced through it again though he had already seen its contents.

"What a wonderful man!" was the gist of what she told Neville Kearney.

On the Thursday the Madrid papers printed a telegram from Berlin reporting the destruction of the aircraft and mentioning the name of Leslie Howard. On that afternoon the Countess Miranda came to Kearney's room in obvious distress. She threw herself down, weeping and blurted forth that she had been acting as a German agent and watching the movements of Leslie Howard in Madrid, *but*, she said, she had done nothing to harm him, and had known nothing of his movements after he had left Spain.

"There was another agent watching him in Lisbon," she sobbed, "and she may be the one who betrayed him."

Neville Kearney spoke a few comforting words, and so ended this poignant encounter.

The reactions in Spain were most marked. Outside in shop windows indignant Spaniards were putting out postcard photos of the film star with black ribbons round them, and the Spanish censor had promptly released the Howard lectures for publication. Articles by Spanish journalists written about his visit, and banned at the time to please the Germans, were now rushed into print. Only after death did his visit have its full propaganda effect.

In Lisbon the businessmen at the Royal British Club stood badly shaken at the bar, and called for another round.

"Yesterday that seagull scene in the film," they muttered, "and he's dead before lunch today."

In Berlin a Goebbels communiqué claimed that the aircraft was "a camouflaged transport aircraft of the DC-3 type". The Germans in neutral capitals said defensively – "anyway, Howard was on a secret mission". For that perhaps they had no more than the word of Countess Miranda.

In Amsterdam, the wives of Tepas, Parmentier, and Verhoeven heard about a Wehrmacht communiqué and then heard the news broadcast by the BBC. None of them knew which crew had been lost.

In London an ambiguous Parliamentary answer was prepared for Sir Archibald Sinclair[1] to read to the House of Commons: "That only one incident has occurred since the service started three years previously shows that no undue risks have been taken."

That was not quite true. At Whitchurch Parmentier sat down to write the last flight report of the *Ibis*, which is the accurate summary of known facts upon which the final explanation may be based.

REPORT ABOUT FLIGHT NO. 777a

On Tuesday, [1 June], the DC-3 G-AGBB left Lisbon Airport for a normal scheduled flight to England, the crew being Captain Q.

Tepas, First Officer D. de Koning, wireless operator C. van Brugge, flight engineer E. Rosevink.

The Duty pilot at Whitchurch, Captain Th. Verhoeven, gave at 09.20 BST the QGO message to the Air Traffic Control Officer at Whitchurch. The weather on the route, according to the forecast would be strong south-westerly wind with rain-showers and the possibility of thunder-storms.

From the message sent by the aircraft we understood that the aircraft had received QGO signal as well as the meteorological forecast which was transmitted by GKH, and that it had left Lisbon 09.35 BST with in total seventeen people on board (thirteen passengers). The machine proceeded perfectly normally, and gave its position in the appropriate way at 10.20, 11.20, and 12.20 BST. His last position was at 44° 509 N. and 09° 509 W.

At 12.54 BST, GKH received a message from G-AGBB saying (in code): 'An unidentified aircraft follows me', and immediately in the same signal, 'I am attacked by enemy aircraft.'

According to the speed of the aircraft the position at 12.54 BST must have been approximately 46° 309 N. and 09° 409 W. GKH immediately replied to G-AGBB, and it kept on calling the aircraft for a long time, but received no further reply.

At 13.20 GMT G-AGBB failed to give its usual position and was considered overdue. At 13.30 Fighter Command asked Coastal Command to send out an aircraft in search for G-AGBB.

It was still possible that the radio of G-AGBB would be out of action and Fighter Command was trying to locate the aircraft with radio location should it approach to the coast, but no aircraft was spotted.

The duty pilot reported at 15.45 BST to the London Management by telephone as well as to the Flying Superintendent, who was on leave. He remained on the airport until 18.00 BST, when the fuel reserve of the aircraft must have been exhausted and no further news of G-AGBB had been received.

If the aircraft would have to land on the water, it would take considerable time to reach the water surface from an altitude of, say, 10,000 feet, and the wireless operator would certainly have used his transmitter if he had been able to do so.

It must therefore be assumed that whilst he was sending out the message, or immediately after, either the radio was out of action or the wireless operator unable to work his radio through being injured by the attack. If this supposition is correct, the aircraft was already hit and damaged simultaneously with the sending out of the message, and therefore the chance of making a safe landing on a very rough sea must be considered very small.

The aircraft was fitted with two rubber dinghies capable of carrying eight people each, and it is understood that from the thirteen passengers, three were children. The dinghies were both properly equipped with first-aid kits, water and food rations, pistols for signals, etc., but it is very doubtful if the crew were able to put out the dinghies.

If the radio was out of action through the attack, it is most likely the crew were killed or injured simultaneously, and it is not impossible that the aircraft would have been either out of control or on fire. In these circumstances the aircraft will have crashed in the sea, and the possibility of using the dinghies for survivors, if any, must be considered very remote.

It is understood that the RAF as well as the Navy have been trying to find survivors at the place where the aircraft was attacked, but also the next day's weather conditions were very unfavourable for a successful air-sea rescue, and up to now there has been no indication that any survivors have been picked up.

Over the Bay of Biscay something was evidently astir the day after the *Ibis* was lost. A Sunderland of 461 Squadron Coastal Command with an Australian crew fought a terrific battle there with eight Junkers 88s, which attacked in a most determined fashion. In one steep dive after another they harried her on her northward flight. After forty-five minutes in running battle low over the waves, the Sunderland limped home to Cornwall with 500 shot-holes in her hull and wing surfaces, and one dying man and four wounded lying on the bomb-room deck. At least three of the Junkers had been shot into the sea.[2]

Then, by contrast, a lull fell on the Bay. The last fierce days of May, the first two days of June were followed by no activity at all. British Coastal Command searched the patrol area for eighteen days without sighting an enemy aircraft. The sky was suddenly empty again.

So the episode seems to end. There was no postwar inquiry on the *Ibis*. Presumption of death was made in all cases, though no trace of wreckage or bodies was ever found. Parmentier wrote to the solicitors of dependents supplying proof of death. He repeated much of what he had said in his first report. He found no reason to alter his conclusions; but he offered no theories for the motive of the attack.

And he got his conference with the Air Ministry at last; he got his astrodomes and exhaust cowlings. Within a week night-flying to Lisbon started. The three surviving planes flew without navigation lights, in wireless silence, with their cabins blacked out,[3] and hooded engine exhausts.

Just one month after the loss of the *Ibis* another encounter was reported, and this proved to be the last. Theo Verhoeven was flying the *Buzzard*. He left Lisbon at 11.25 p.m. on 1 July on the homeward flight, with ten passengers on board. *Buzzard* was at a height of

11,000 feet in the early darkness of the next day, flying nearly due north, when they saw an amber light.[4]

"At that time I noticed an amber light moving in the same direction," said Verhoeven. "The light was above the layer of cirrus cloud that covered the sea. I estimated its height at 4–5,000 feet above sea level. The light made a peculiar zig-zagging movement. It was still too dark to see the plane."

He remembered a British pilot telling him of an amber light sighted the previous night over the Bay.

"Do you see it?" he asked Otten, his First Officer.

"Yes," answered Otten, his head in the darkened astrodrome. "But I can't see the plane."

The amber light kept on its parallel course, below them, a ghostly companion over the moonlit cirrus of Biscay.

Verhoeven swung the *Buzzard* hard round on to a course of 70° West and for fifteen minutes he flew on that bearing in a zig-zag pattern. They lost sight of the amber light for about five minutes. Then it appeared again for a short time, and finally vanished altogether.

It was carried by a radar-fitted night fighter. This is of interest in estimating German intentions at that time. The Dutch crews saw no more lights of any kind after that flight. Nor was there any other incident on the Lisbon line. A year later the Allies landed in Normandy, and the Germans withdrew headlong from the Bordeaux area. They abandoned their airfields, the U-boat pens, their barracks. Army Group G, Air Fleet III, and Admiral Commanding U-boats went into retreat together, with the *maquis* rising behind them.

It was no longer necessary for the Lisbon route to be flown so far west. It resumed direct flights by day from Lisbon to Hurn, and then to Whitchurch, flying straight over the Breton peninsula instead of the Isles of Scilly. The sense of danger was past. The Bay was cleared of the enemy, but the incident of Flight 777 was never explained, even by the interrogation of Luftwaffe personnel. At this point we seek the conclusive evidence. Over to the enemy!

Chapter 21

The Case for the Luftwaffe

First, to find the survivors of the German squadrons which had fought in France in 1943 and 1944; but in those Luftwaffe fighter formations which were involved in the Normandy battle the casualties had been enormously high. Would there be any survivors who remembered that faraway incident in the Bay of Biscay?

What was the German formation most likely to have taken part in the air battles over Biscay in 1943? At the end of the war there had been living in retirement in Westphalia an interesting Colonel of the Luftwaffe called Theo Rowehl. He had been a close friend of Admiral Canaris, Chief of German Military Intelligence Services. In fact, he had commanded a Special Air Reconnaissance Squadron, which had worked all over Europe, map-making in advance of the German Wehrmacht. I located him eventually in the Ruhr, and a slow train took me to the town where Colonel Rowehl had settled. An elderly, white-haired man with a thoughtful, deliberate manner greeted me at the door of his flat. There I sat and first listened to the story of the Rowehl Circus.

"I was in the Imperial Navy with Canaris," he began, "and transferred to the Luftwaffe, but my squadron existed before there was ever an established Luftwaffe. For you do not need fighter aircraft for air reconnaissance. Small sports planes will do.

"It was our practice to photograph twice yearly along the frontiers of Germany from the early thirties. How did we do it? We took advantage of broken cloud, or we trusted that the French and the Czechs would fail to notice us. Sometimes we would tow a long sleeve behind us advertising chocolate as we photographed. Sometimes on the Baltic coast we towed a target sleeve for naval gunnery practice, and as we made our target runs we photographed the whole of the Polish corridor coastal fortifications.

"The photographs were compared with those taken six months previously. They showed the growth of the enemy defences. Often we ventured right over the Maginot line without interference.

"During the war, from my base in Oranienburg, I worked in an ever-widening spiral with forward bases at Aalberg, Kirkenes, Simferopol, Crete, Bordeaux …"

"Ah, Bordeaux," I interrupted. "Then you will have done reconnaissance over the Biscay area and along the coast of Spain?"

"Yes."

"Did you know of the incident in 1943 when a civil airliner was shot down on the Lisbon route?"

"I heard about it. Does it interest you?"

I said that it did, and Theo Rowehl began to recall what he knew.

He was not of the opinion that it was easy for the Germans to intercept the airliners of the Lisbon route. To begin with, there had been an agreement – a gentleman's agreement – not to attack the Stockholm planes, and a common interest existed in the Lisbon traffic. It carried newspapers, contraband, air mail.

"But as the war went on and became more bitter, without special instructions from above a less tolerant view would be taken."

He had heard the rumours that the Luftwaffe were after Churchill when they shot down the *Ibis*. His own squadron operated independently, seconded to Intelligence, and it had no orders either to intercept or shadow the Lisbon airliners. His aircraft were unarmed. He knew of the orders to assassinate Churchill, but he did not think they were issued as early as 1943. He thought that they were first seriously considered in 1944 – on that point his memory was vague and his words few.

"What Luftwaffe formation was operating then over Biscay?" I asked.

"It was a mixed fighter wing called Kampfgruppe 40," he replied.

I noted the name, noted also that an old comrades' magazine for the Luftwaffe had just started publication. So I sent in a small advertisement for its personal columns to the "Luftwaffenring". It read: "Survivors of KG.40 are sought for historical research purposes."

Three weeks later I had a reply from a radio operator. He wrote on a postcard in a neat round script: "I served with Major Hemm in KG.40, and would be glad to answer your questions." It was signed Peter Friedlein. I motored over to Franconia and woke Friedlein out of a Sunday afternoon nap, and it was he who gave me the only eyewitness account in existence of the shooting down of the *Ibis*. But by the time I came to question him another important piece of evidence had been discovered – the official German report on the incident.

A war historian, prompted by myself and by occasional inquiries from the Howard family, had been searching enemy documents without result. He had in fact given up looking in captured enemy documents and was about to make his answer "an informed guess", when, reading the German Atlantic archives, so he told me, he discovered a Luftwaffe paper inserted loose among the other reports.

"This has, I am glad to say," the historian wrote, "produced new evidence which enables us to establish the identity of the Luftwaffe unit concerned with a fair degree of certainty."

This evidence shows that eight Junkers 88s took off at 10.00 hours on 1 June 1943, probably from Kerhouin-Bastard airfield, their tasks being air-sea rescue and protection of two U-boats. They failed to sight the U-boats, and as the weather was unfavourable for search work, they may have been on their way back to base when at 12.45 a transport aircraft, described in the German report as a DC-3, was sighted, flying on a north-easterly course. She was attacked five minutes later (the report mentions six attacks), caught fire and dived into the sea. Four men were observed to jump from the aircraft, but no mention is made of any search for survivors.

Unless you have any evidence to the contrary, it would appear likely that this was the aircraft in which Leslie Howard was travelling.

The German aircraft on this operation were Junkers 88 C.6s the fighter version, and this pinpoints the unit as the fifth squadron of Fighter Group KG.40.

We have no records of the names of the crews on the actual operation, but you may be interested to know that the CO of the squadron was a Major Alfred Hemm who, as far as I can trace, survived the war.

Thus the name Alfred Hemm came up twice in quick succession. At last the pieces were fitting together. It would undoubtedly be worthwhile to talk to the radio operator who had served under him in KG.40.

In a half-timbered Franconian farmhouse a short, thickset man of about thirty, of peasant stock, with a round red face, sat up, stared, and rubbed his eyes.

"You are Peter Friedlein, the radio operator who answered my advertisement about Fighter Group 40?" I asked him.

He nodded expectantly, "I would like to get in touch with my Commanding Officer, Major Hemm. Do you know where he is?"

I replied that I too wanted very much to meet Major Hemm, but perhaps he could help me in the meantime. Did he remember a transport aircraft, an airliner, being shot down over the Bay of Biscay in the summer of 1943?

"Yes, I remember quite clearly," said Peter Friedlein. "I was there."

He pulled out an old Luftwaffe map from his bookshelf, spread it on the table, and moved a stubby finger along the parallels.

"The time was about noon," he said. "The position near forty-six degrees North and zero-nine degrees West."

That was almost exactly the last position of the *Ibis*, according to the reckoning of Parmentier.

"Can you tell me what happened?" I inquired.

"It was the end of May or the beginning of June," said Peter Friedlein. "Our *Staffel* was on patrol from Lorient in Brittany. I suppose I've been in a hundred patrols in the Biscay and Channel area. Our practice was to fly out in echelon to latitude fourteen degrees West and then work to a chessboard pattern southwards.

"If we located crippled U-boats, we gave them umbrella. On these patrols we have fought Liberators, Whitleys, Sunderlands, Catalinas, Lancasters, Wellington, and Halifax bombers.

"I remember that day. The Bay was rough. There was a high wind, low cloud, and below the cloud it looked misty, with bad visibility. We came out of cloud, at the tail-end of our patrol, and it was Flight Lieutenant Bellstedt of Bremen, I think, who sighted the aircraft in the sun, flying a northerly course, perhaps a thousand or a thousand-five-hundred metres above the overcast.

"Lieutenant Bellstedt was in a good position to attack, and he went in at once. It was over very quickly. My aircraft, the second in the third pair, did not have time to attack. By then the airliner was diving steeply and in flames."

Peter Friedlein hesitated, as if something was troubling him. His narrative became more abrupt. His face clouded as he spoke.

"All sorts of stuff was thrown out. I remember people jumping in desperation. I think there was a parachute. She was still above the cloud then. She dived through the cloud, but I did not see her hit the sea. I did not see the end."

"Didn't you look for survivors?"

"We'd been out a long time, and we were not minded to stooge about."

"Didn't you follow down through the cloud?"

"Well, we followed the others down, but there was bad visibility and we saw nothing.

"I'm not sure what instructions Lieutenant Bellstedt had when he attacked the airliner. There was a lot of talk when we got back to base because we had shot down a civil aircraft.[1] Lieutenant Bellstedt is dead now. All the officers of that flight were killed; but there was no disciplining of Lieutenant Bellstedt. At least, I didn't know of any."

I asked whether Bellstedt[2] was in touch with base before shooting down the airliner.

"I think he went in to attack immediately, because the aircraft was so close and right in the sun, so he couldn't see the markings," replied Friedlein.

This reply seemed to me of doubtful value, because the Hemm report, of which Friedlein evidently knew nothing, says that five minutes elapsed between sighting the aircraft and the first attack.[3]

"If I'd been the Allied pilot I wouldn't have flown so high above the cloud," said Friedlein. "He hadn't time to dive a thousand metres. If he'd been skimming the clouds it would have been different."

I learned this much more from Peter Friedlein. Lieutenant Bellstedt had been shot down over Germany; another officer flying that day in the second pair, Pilot Officer Neccsany, had been killed over the Bay of Biscay soon afterwards by a shot in the head. He had managed to pancake his aircraft on the sea before he died. A British flying-boat, thought Friedlein, or air-sea rescue craft, came in and captured his radio operator and observer floating in a rubber dinghy.

This information fits in with an RAF report that one of these two survivors volunteered the explanation while still fresh from the sea that they "had shot down that airliner for target practice", whereas he was promptly beaten up by the British rescue crew, and in consequence would say not a word more when officially interrogated about the incident.

It seemed essential to discover a German officer of senior rank to dispose of these conflicting reports. I asked who then was the Commodore of the Bordeaux Coastal Group in 1943, and was told that it was Colonel Robert Kowalewski.[4] He had survived the war, was living in West Germany, but at first did not react to my letters. The telephone exchange traced his number, and after some talk with his wife, it was arranged that I should see the demurring Commodore. At last an officer who must know the truth of the matter; for of Alfred Hemm there was no sign, and the radio operator Friedlein was perhaps not in a position to know why the patrol had been flown at that time in that area, or what instructions were given to the officers.

Colonel Robert Kowalewski, Commodore of Fighter Group 40 in 1943, was a broad-shouldered, curly-headed man, much scarred about the forehead, and with a peculiar mark under his chin from a spent bullet that had passed between his knees and ended up in his mouth as he flew over the east coast of Scotland in 1941. He came warily to meet me.

"If it is about Group Forty, I can tell you what I know," said Kowalewski, and he led the way up to the top flat, where his blonde wife was setting a small table.

It was a spacious flat with beautiful rugs. On the polished table lay a dark blue bollard-like object, too massive to have been designed as an ashtray – the purpose that it was serving. I picked it up – it was a mast top, the splintered stem of the mast still in it.

"Got stuck in my tail-wing," said Kowalewski, "as I was flying through one of your convoys."

Kowalewski had been Commodore of Coastal Group 40 from summer 1941 to autumn 1943 – the entire period that interested me. He told me the story of KG.40 from the beginning. I did not hurry him. He would come eventually to the points that interested me.

"Coastal Group Forty, or KG.Forty, as we called it," said Kowalewski, "was formed by General Jeschonnek, Chief of Air Staff, in March nineteen-forty-one. He wanted to use it as the counterpart to your Coastal Command, and he laid down that it was to consist entirely of four-engined aircraft. First it was to be Heinkel 177s, but they never came. Instead we received Condors, Dornier 217s, and finally Junkers 88.

"The Führer Headquarters kept on snatching the Condors for the Reich Courier Squadron. It was in fact a converted civil aircraft, not really fast; it had to be flown carefully till it settled down, being lightly built; but it had a long range and could stay up for sixteen hours at a time. Bordeaux to Norway was an easy patrol for the Condor.

"Then there was the Junkers 88, with only seven hours' flying and a range no further than twelve-to-thirteen degrees West, but of course it was more heavily armed.

"Now the wings of KG.40 lay thus:

I Wing, Condors in Bordeaux to patrol over Biscay.
II Wing, Dorniers in Soesterberg, Holland, for North Sea patrol.
III Wing, Heinkels in Rennes, Brittany, for Channel patrol.

IV Wing, at Chateaudun, for convoy warfare between Thames and Tyne.

V   Wing, Junkers 88, at Lorient, commanded by Major Alfred Hemm and directly under Naval Command West for the U-boat war."

"It is Wing Five that interests me," I said.

Kowalewski went on, "I recollect that Wing used to try and intercept British stripped-down fighters being flown high at night to Malta in 1942 for equipment and arming out there.

"Now to come to the point about your inquiry. I, as Commodore of KG.40, had no instructions either way about airliners using the Lisbon route. I knew no times of flight, and I expected them to vary their route and fly at irregular intervals.

"I have looked at my log book, and I see that on 2 June 1943, I myself flew an eleven-hour patrol thirteen degrees West at top alert on watch for British bombers. I believe that Naval Command West was very worried at that time about a blockade runner approaching Bordeaux from the Azores area with a cargo of raw rubber from Malaya. For five or six days at the beginning of June we flew day and night with orders to shoot on sight any aircraft. We were at the top state of alert.

"I remember that a few days after the DC-3 was shot down I received a list of the passengers. There was a great fuss about it all. I recall that the name of Leslie Howard was among them.

"I couldn't answer for everything that happened while I was Commodore at KG.40," said Kowalewski heavily, "but I'll answer for the case of this airliner. Let me try and find Major Hemm for you and inquire what was the sequel."

Months later I received a letter from Kowalewski.

I have asked the Intelligence Staff Officer of Air Officer Commanding Atlantic [he wrote]. A report on the case went up to Air Fleet III in Paris. As the crews were young and inexperienced, there was no official court of inquiry, and the incident was booked as an error of judgement. I have been unable to find Major Hemm, so I do not see that I can do anything more.

So the elusive Hemm could not be found.[5] There would probably be no fresh evidence now. I was left wondering very much whether, if Winston Churchill had been flying in that aircraft, the shooting down would still have been booked as an "error of judgement".

Chapter 22

Curtain

The mortals have ended their quarrels for the time being. Their towers of spray, their climbing tracer shells illumine the Bay no longer. The tides, the winds, the currents rehearse their ceaseless pattern undisturbed. On the Biscay shelf or in the Atlantic deep lie the twisted spars of the aircraft that fought this phase of the Battle of the Atlantic, the British flying-boats that hugged the waves in running combat with their armoured backs ablaze at the diving German fighters in the area named in operations 'Derange'. Somewhere among them lie the bones of the *Ibis*.

Too little has been written about this strange war of air-to-sea and air-to-air, with the radar bombers dipping out of the cloud at night to straddle the U-boats with depth-charges. It was a secret war at the time, and much of it has remained unknown since.

But we are still in quest of certainty about one episode, and here I must endeavour to sift the evidence and find the answer. Was Flight 777 intercepted simply because the Germans knew Leslie Howard was on board? I do not think so, because there is absolutely no trace in any surviving document or interrogation report to that effect. There is only hearsay.

Was the Luftwaffe after the Jewish agent, Wilfrid Israel? Again I am inclined to doubt it, because in the prevailing weather it was a hit-or-miss operation. Moreover, his name is not mentioned either in the only surviving German document.

Was the Hemm report on this incident perhaps a plant, concocted after the event to conceal a deliberate attack on a civil aircraft? The Air Ministry tells me "there is no reason to doubt its accuracy". If it had been doctored to cover up a crime against a civil airliner, it would probably have suggested, as the radio operator Peter Friedlein did in his conversation with me, that the encounter was quite sudden, and that the *Ibis* was shot down by a pilot partially blinded by the sun. Whereas the Hemm report makes it plain that the *Ibis* was first shadowed for at least five minutes by the German fighters, so that the attack must have been deliberate. The Hemm report is honest in that.

Is the conclusion, then, that this attack, though deliberate, was a pure mischance? I would not agree to that, nor yet accept the explanation of the German commodore that these sorties were flown solely for the protection of a blockade runner trying to approach Bordeaux with a cargo of rubber from the Far East.

For the Board of Admiralty, after long research on my behalf among captured enemy naval documents, assures me that it is quite certain that no blockade runner at all was approaching Biscay in that week. So we are left to wonder why, apart from the U-boat war, there was a general alert of the Luftwaffe in the Biscay area for four or five days at the beginning of June, and why Colonel Kowalewski flew hour after hour in darkness so far west, and why the Junkers 88s attacked that Sunderland flying-boat with the Australian crew next day with such tremendous persistence as she was flying north.

I tend to the conclusion that the state of top alert lasting about a week over the Bay of Biscay was maintained for one purpose. The reason, in my view, was indeed the presence of Winston Churchill in Algeria, due to fly home at any moment.[1] Who knows how close the weaving amber light of Colonel Kowalewski in his Condor may have got to the Prime Minister's Boeing in the darkness of the wide sweep westwards?[2]

Here again we have no documentary evidence of a 'Kill Churchill' order, only hearsay. But the rumour was afoot in Lisbon that he would pass that way, and uncertainty about one foundered U-boat, U-263, could not have led to such a prolonged strafe over the Bay as lasted five days. Nor was it necessary for the German Air Command to specify the target, as long as it ordered day and night patrols and all strange aircraft to be shot down. In fact such secrecy was probably desirable. Only by long vigilance and prolonged patrols could it hope to shoot down such a prize as Churchill. It would not have been possible, even with the best intelligence, to clock his departure and pinpoint his aircraft. So a wide net was spread in those days, and a high state of alert maintained.

It is impossible also to ignore the two previous attacks that had been made on the *Ibis*, though probably not pressed home with the same determination as the third. The first of these may well have been a case of mistaken identity by a single aircraft.

There is also, for those whom it may interest, the natural reason, and the supernatural. My studies of this incident suggest how small indeed, even in war, is the human agency, compared to the vastness of the sky, the accidents of cloud and wind, the moving hands of time, and the higher rulings. Was it perhaps determined in advance that on Flight 777 the luck of the *Ibis* would forsake her, and all who flew with her were to perish?

Yet intermingled with it you still have the human agents, increasing the coincidence of factors that led to this decisive encounter; Tepas deciding to fly above cloud, Leslie Howard hurrying back to fetch a package from the Customs at Portela, and so delaying the plane by five minutes. Those five minutes were fifteen miles lost in flying time; that would perhaps have put a safety distance between the *Ibis* and the enemy.

So you could say, if you like, that it was a gift for the Denham ladies that caused the loss of the *Ibis;* or an argument between pilots on the use of cloud; or departmental slowness in releasing astrodomes; or the determination of the Dutch not to give up flying.

The most curious thing, to my mind, was that Leslie Howard should walk into this picture. He was the only one who could have flown home exactly when he chose. He had both priority and individuality; and he evidently chose to fly that day for no reason that we can more than guess at. Until the day before he had been, if anything, tending to prolong his visit, as if in search of something new and unusual.

It was as if the scene was set for him to mount a new film; the characters assembled in Lisbon, the glitter, colour, and mystery of a brush with the enemy in neutral territory. Had his impulses led him to wait for a day, he would have seen the whole drama from offstage, and made of it, surely, his finest wartime film. But at the last moment the producer chose to step in among the actors. Unlike him, to make an unlucky decision!

What of the other characters? Parmentier was lost in an accident in fog after the war. Verhoeven captained 1316 RAF (Dutch) Transport Flight which served between London and Leyden in 1945 until normal air traffic was restored. He returned to the battered Schiphol and his wife in their little redbrick villa by the canal. Dik, Alsem and others of the gallant Dutch fliers in Bristol returned to their peacetime flying with KLM.

The mechanics, crews, and ground staff who had worked together at Whitchurch scattered to new duties, some of them married Bristol girls and some went back to Holland and their families. You cannot travel far by air today without meeting British and Dutchmen who flew the Lisbon route, but none of them feels positively able to say what strange touch of coincidence brought down *Ibis* over the Bay of Biscay.

What became of Countess Miranda? It does not appear that the Gestapo took effective action against her. She did not return to the Third Reich. The British agent may well have found a use for her and given her protection in Madrid. At the end of the war she changed her nationality by marriage. Occasionally she comes to Europe. You can see her sometimes among the fashionable crossbred society that winters at St Moritz and Cannes, sits about Rome, and is in Paris for the season, but seldom if ever comes to London. She is still remarkably beautiful. I wonder if she ever thinks today that she was once sent to spy for Hitler in Spain, or recalls the pale, calm face of the man whom she thought was on a British secret mission.

By chance I met her once before completing this book. It was in a mansion that she had rented in Seville for Holy Week. I reminded her of wartime days and the story of Leslie Howard.

"I was never blacklisted by the Allies," she said, "but the British and American diplomats in Madrid always wanted to know with whom I had been dining. Yes, I met Leslie Howard once at a party. Who can say why he was shot down?"

And what became of the children of Israel? His plans for the young people to return to their national home seemed to be shattered by his death, as all the threads had been in his hands. Five months afterwards another representative of the Jewish agency arrived in Lisbon, searching for the lists of names that might have perished in the aircraft. He found that Wilfrid Israel had taken the precaution of leaving copies in the offices of the Quaker Mission and the American Jewish Joint Distribution Committee, and so the organisation began again its stealthy activities.

The French *maquis* and Spanish agents brought the Jewish children across the Pyrenees by night. With forged papers, fugitives from France, Holland, and Belgium were drafted into the Todt Labour Organisation, sent to work on fortifications near the frontier, and smuggled across into Spain.

Between January 1944 and the end of the war in Europe, 2,600 refugees had sailed to Palestine in the Portuguese ships *Niasu, Guine,* and *Lima,* the Spanish steamship *Plus Ultra* and a British ship plying from Gibraltar.

So the dream of Israel was accomplished, though not with spades and hoes, as he had last seen them. The young men whom he had rescued from one war fought another against those who had helped to liberate them. That was a bitter thing. This conflict in loyalties was spared to Wilfrid Israel.

No wonder that this many-hued spray arose from the loss of the *Ibis* and that the legend has not since subsided. It will never be entirely easy to see it as an ordinary accident, an ordinary act of war, or an aircraft that just flew into trouble.

When giants are moving about the world, even the slightest incidents can become momentous. We look for a pattern, a design, an explanation for everything. It is hard to accept the whim, the freak of coincidence, or the plain accident, when you are working in a neutral capital in the fever of intelligence.

In time of war the more dramatic picture is the more credible to us. We see the bald and pertinacious Germans sitting like automatons at their Staff desks, reporting, commanding, perspiring, and achieving. It did not then seem at all beyond the vaunted efficiency of Hitler and his High Command to come near to killing Churchill and destroying another aircraft instead. The enemy, while his grandiose aims are still not frustrated, is an apparition of tentacular power and superhuman cunning. Only afterwards do we see the full scope of the enemy's failings and how many of his interlocking devices failed to respond to the touch. Finally, searching in the rubble for the colossus, all we find of him is a rag, a bone, and a hank of hair. His commanders, his planners, his spies become shrunken, loquacious, and unshaven internees. The spell is broken.

To sum up, the possibilities are that German Intelligence became even more interested in Leslie Howard when they had heard Countess Miranda's story about him. That would explain why they reported on him as a British agent. It is quite possible that a report about Winston Churchill passing through Lisbon was purposely spread about to deceive the enemy as to his time of flying and true route over the dangerous Bay of Biscay. The Germans must have known about the activities of Wilfrid Israel, probably also of Ivan Sharp and Shervington, and so this passenger list was not without interest, though in fact it was much more important to see to the Luftwaffe radar and fighter net over the whole Bay and beyond.

Of course there was anxiety in England about the return of the Prime Minister – there always was – but here I switch the scene to Brisbane late in 1944 and let the final episode be told by an intelligence officer from the Supreme Headquarters of the Allied Expeditionary Force to Europe. He had been sent out to lecture on secrecy to officers of the Task Force mounted in Australia for the invasion of Japan.

He impressed on them the importance of surprise in an invasion, and the necessity of knowing everything the enemy was doing. The enemy signals system must be tapped and deciphered, and up to the last moment, when wireless silence starts, and even after that, there must be no clue given to the enemy that his signals are overheard.

To emphasise this point, he said, he could relate the strange case of an Allied airliner shot down on the Lisbon route a year previously. The Allied listening net was spread from Britain to tap the whole enemy-occupied coast from Norway to Spain, giving an incomparable picture of the nervous system of the Germans, and their actions and reactions. It was supplying an accurate forecast of enemy movements which Allied generals and field marshals writing their memoirs later would doubtless be permitted to ascribe to their own prescience – in reality it was the mosaic of thousands of minds.

Among the intercepted messages, the Brisbane lecturer declared, there was one from a German transmitter in Lisbon on 31 May showing some interest in the passengers flying from Lisbon to London on the following day. Their names were being reported to Berlin.

Ought this to be regarded as a special case, the interceptors asked themselves? Such reports had been sometimes overheard by the Allies before. But at this moment there was special activity over the Bay, and the Prime Minister was expected home. Should the aircraft be held up or those passengers mentioned taken off it? One paramount consideration overruled any such suggestion. It was deemed likely that no such step could be taken without a risk of it becoming known that an enemy source of information was being tapped. That would lead to enemy wireless silence in Lisbon, the picture would become blurred, the mastery of intelligence might be lost. It was decided at the top, so I am told by an officer who was present at the lecture, that no action was to be taken. And so the *Ibis* flew.[3]

It may even be that the antennae of Allied intelligence, working from obscure country houses in the Home Counties, heard on the air the credulous German reports, and realised – with a degree of apprehension – that a floating rumour of Churchill visiting Lisbon on his way home had become an accepted fact to German Intelligence. This would explain the interest of both sides in any aircraft that was flying out of Lisbon next day, and the forty-five minute battle with the Sunderland.

I am not able to give official confirmation of this account, but it seems to offer an explanation for the instant assumption afterwards that the *Ibis* had been singled out and shot down deliberately in mistake for Churchill's plane – even if that intent is still not proven. If this story is true, it adds something to the consoling reflection of Mrs Chenhalls when she told Mrs Churchill that, of their husbands, "England could best spare mine". For it is a fact that Allied intelligence remained supreme, and when the Normandy invasion started every German move was known. It might not have been so in June 1944 if the rules of silence had been broken or the gossip of the air revealed in June 1943 even to a small circle in a neutral capital.

So whatever the sure hand of fate, the sporadic dispositions of men, and the quirks of coincidence had to do with the loss of the *Ibis*, I believe that such a decision on secrecy was justified and that Leslie Howard and his companions would have understood it.

Postscript

Andrew Colvin

Ever since Icarus, air accidents have always provoked curiosity way beyond the relatively small number of people who die in them compared with the number killed on roads. Having finally convinced ourselves on take-off that these heavy beasts can actually fly, we also find it difficult to understand why they crash on the unfortunate occasions that this happens. The Second World War produced a number of air incident mysteries which have invited all sorts of conspiracy theories without receiving any clear answers.

There was the saga of Rudolf Hess and his ambiguous journey to Scotland. In June 1940 there was the shooting down at Tobruk of the Italian air ace and Governor of Libya, Marshal Italo Balbo, just eighteen days after Italy's declaration of war, to which he had been vigorously opposed. In 1942 Prince George of Kent was killed when a Sunderland flying-boat crashed into a Scottish hillside, in circumstances which were obscure and inadequately investigated. Then in 1943 there was Flight 777, the subject of this book, followed on 4 July 1943, by the death of General Sikorski, the Polish Prime Minister in exile, shortly after take-off from Gibraltar.

In deciding to republish this book, we approached the subject with open minds to see how Ian Colvin's work had stood the passage of time, the subsequent revealing of some information which was secret in the 1950s and investigations made by others since. Our analysis was that it was remarkably accurate. Colvin's conclusion was that of an open verdict, but with a number of unanswered questions. He was clear that there had been an order for the Luftwaffe to intensify operations on account of Churchill's visit to North Africa and return to Britain, but did not subscribe to the theory of mistaken identity of Chenhalls. Whether that intensification order was to include civilian planes has not been explained but if, as alleged, the rumour that Churchill was to pass via Lisbon and even use a civilian flight reached Germany, then it would have been logical to extend the net.

Some survivors of the Luftwaffe air crew protested their innocence, in the sense that this civilian plane G-AGBB was not considered by them the specific target of a planned attack. Thanks to the work of Ben Rosevink and Chris Goss, contact was made again with aircrew, though Hintze had not been interviewed before and was not mentioned by Colvin. Having read the reports, documents and copy correspondence kindly lent by Rosevink, and allowing for a number of inconsistencies and approximations, it seems quite likely that Hintze and Friedlein were being truthful to the best of their recollections. However, that is not the end of the story. Colvin seems to have been fobbed off with Robert Kowalewski as a substitute for Major Hemm, the man most likely to have given any direct line order. Colvin's investigations took place at a time when the incident of shooting down this civilian plane could have been indicted as a war crime, and one would understand Hemm's reluctance.

What emerges is that, although Hintze claims that he led the squadron that day (contrary to Colvin's account), Bellstedt and Wittmer-Eigenbrodt were the pilots of the two higher-level spotter planes, and it was Bellstedt who led the dive into attack. Whether others followed his example is really a side issue. On the basis of the information available to date, we simply do not know whether Bellstedt had received any instructions from Hemm which were not disclosed to the rest of the squadron, or whether he was in radio contact with base. Nor do we know on what basis the flight plan was devised that would bring the squadron into the quadrant of airspace at the same time as the *Ibis*, though Ronald Howard's information was that the planes on the Lisbon run had been regularly sighted by the Germans in the past.

No evidence has been found, or has survived, of instructions targeting the *Ibis*, yet there are still many matters which just refuse to go away, both in relation to the flight and to Leslie Howard's mission. The catalogued files on Howard are no longer closed, but it is believed that there are still some previously uncatalogued Security Service files to be released as well as copy documents which may be found elsewhere.

The qualities of several of the passengers might have justified, in German eyes, an attack. For some passengers, their work was over so it would have been more a matter for vindictive satisfaction than a major step in the war; for Howard, Israel and, perhaps, Shervington nothing was over. Was there someone who was expected to be on the plane who did not in fact board? We do not know the names transmitted to Germany on the afternoon of Monday 31 May in that this communication has not been made available, and there is conflict between the different accounts. Father Holmes was taken off, but when? There are at least two versions. Then there is the uncorroborated assertion that Foley, an officer of MI6, should have been on that flight.

Colvin's inclination was that Leslie Howard was not a deliberate target. Whether or not that is right, there remain questions about Howard's mission. Despite Roosevelt's 'unconditional surrender' edict, contacts with German intelligence were taking place in the Iberian Peninsula; Howard's role would not have been for traditional espionage or gathering of intelligence, but he could have opened some sensitive negotiation. Another strand came to light with the publication by José Rey-Ximena of *El Vuolo de Ibis*, claiming that Conchita Montenegro used her influence and contacts to introduce Howard to Generalissimo Franco, thus contributing to keeping Spain out of the war. If that were the mission, it might explain some of the nervousness of Howard at the prospect of going to Spain. Keeping Spain out of the war was an important goal, pursued by many in Madrid, but would that have been the only item on the agenda? There is no trace elsewhere of any meeting between Howard and Franco; if it did take place in all the chaotic friction generated between Starkie and his guest, then Leslie Howard would have been a far cleverer operator than the distracted, vague image would credit. Yet there is one curious detail: the picture of Conchita Montenegro appears in the original edition, but she is not mentioned once in the text. Was there an objection on her part? The Countess Miranda is not a proper substitute and seems an amalgam of several women.

Colvin concludes with the consideration of the intercepted message and what is the proper reaction on being alerted to something which could have catastrophic consequences for the persons affected. Whilst a message could well have indicated a suitable target, who knew how that would have been processed through the German system and whether it would have been translated into an order to attack? The *Ultra* decrypting of German radio messages was a vital defensive weapon in the war. Its secret was to be protected at all costs. In his final paragraph Colvin summed up the moral dilemma that faced the decision makers about a weapon whose very existence remained an official secret until 1974.

* * *

Since writing the above postscript, some further details can be added. Whilst they do not decide the issue as to whether the attack was a deliberate target, or whether there was a decision not to act on the information apparently received through an *Enigma* intercept, they raise questions as to what various people, and particularly British intelligence, thought they were doing in the Iberian theatre. Of three names which need no introduction, Kim Philby, Graham Greene and Guy Burgess, Philby and Greene had responsibility for disinformation in Iberia, whilst Burgess was involved in obtaining the necessary authorisation from the Ministry of Information for Chenhalls to travel. As for Chenhalls, his sister Joan Chenhalls MBE, was a member of MI5, which may have made the mistaken identity story rather easier. Then there was the presence in Portugal of Foley of MI6. Was he instrumental in the 'bumping' of Derek Partridge, son of an MI6 man in Washington from that 1 June flight, and also perhaps an intervention in favour of Father Holmes? All this leads to the elusive key question whether Leslie Howard had a broader mission in his visit, with negotiating contacts which would not have been possible outside the Iberian neutrality.

Notes

Chapter 1

1. The author was correspondent for the *Sunday Times* in Germany after the war and followed some of the Nuremberg trials.
2. Reproduced by kind permission of Cassell and Co. Ltd.
3. See *Chief of Intelligence*, Ch. XIX.
4. One of these was likely to have been Frank Foley who travelled to Portugal a number of times in 1942 and 1943. Foley had before the War managed the Passport Office in Berlin as well as working for MI6. His role meant that he could not be mentioned in the credits in the Foreword. Other possibilities were Douglas Brown, correspondent in Lisbon for the *Times* 1935–42 and for Reuters 1942 until his expulsion in 1946, and Cedric Salter, a journalist who had previously covered the Spanish civil war.
5. Ronald Howard later went on to write *In Search of my Father*, published in 1981.
6. Nickname, based on his guffawing voice, usually associated, though not exclusively, with William Joyce, who enlisted in the cause of German propaganda. He was tried and hanged, controversially, for treason in 1946.

Chapter 2

1. No doubt seconded by the adverse report sent by Walter Starkie of the British Institute and British Council in Madrid, who referred to 'undesirable elements' attracted by the tour. Quoted in Eforgan, *Leslie Howard, The Lost Actor*, p.223.
2. Canaris had a far wider freedom to travel than almost anyone else in Germany up until 1944, from Baghdad to Lisbon; see Colvin, *Chief of Intelligence*.
3. As this came from the Portuguese customs, it can be taken as the list 'as flown', with changes as compared to the 'final list' closed on Saturday 29 May, quoted in R. Howard, *In Search of my Father*, p.210. Colvin does not give a complete list of the subsequent changes made on Monday, 31 May, noting only the inclusion of Howard and Chenhalls and the removal of

Father Holmes. At the time of boarding, rather than a list, Colvin reconstructed a narrative of welcoming on board all the passengers, corresponding to the Portuguese list.

4. In support of the theory of mistaken identity for Churchill, some have noted a similarity between Howard and Walter H. Thompson, personal assistant to Churchill – see blogger.com El Viaje de Leslie.

5. His son duly became a pilot in the RAF, but was killed on a bombing mission in 1944.

6. No source is given here. Who could the passenger have been who was taken off? Would a secretary to the Cuban consulate in Liverpool have had priority over that passenger?

Chapter 3

1. The route to Lisbon was towards the upper end of the DC-3's range, so that it is unlikely that she would take so many passengers, and it is understood that the *Ibis* was actually fitted out with just fourteen passenger seats. Then there was also some freight to be carried.

2. A criticism made by Herbert Hintze, one of the German crew interviewed by Ben Rosevink (to whom we are indebted for the sight of correspondence), was that the camouflage gave a military appearance to the DC-3. Whilst this could protect it when parked on an airfield, it was of little use when flying a predominantly maritime route. By 1943 the shape could be confused with the military version, the C-47 or Dakota, but at the time of camouflaging that was not a problem since the C-47 was not yet to be seen in the skies. Howard asserts that *Ibis* was painted duck-egg blue; this is unlikely overall, but was common for the aircraft belly – see www.classicwarbirds.co.uk. Friedlein, the other German pilot Rosevink was able to interview, noted that civilian aircraft on the Berlin–Madrid and Berlin–Stockholm routes were painted bright red, which would remove any excuse of ambiguity. Rosevink's investigations, also in search of the father he never knew, led to a joint article with Hintze in *Flypast*, No.120, July 1991.

Chapter 4

1. Eforgan has more detail on the history of 'Her Cardboard Lover'. Apparently the first leading lady was actually Laurette Taylor. She shared with her successors a difficulty in managing alcohol. *Leslie Howard, The Lost Actor*, p. 63 et seq.

2. More outrageous behaviour described in Eforgan, op. cit. pp. 66–72.
3. No film of that title appears in the repertory of Howard films. The juxtaposition of the reference to Nevile Henderson suggests that Colvin thought of the latter as the lost man, which was the impression also from their encounters described in *The Chamberlain Cabinet*, but it is not clear whether Howard was also thinking along the same lines. However, the outline later of his plans to the Ministry of Information suggests that Howard had indeed studied the character of Nevile Henderson.

Chapter 5

1. British Ambassador in Berlin until the outbreak of war, his pursuit of appeasement policy was often at variance with others on the staff, as well as the MI6 officer, Frank Foley. For more detail see Colvin. *The Chamberlain Cabinet*.
2. Englishman describes only one façade of this complex character, of US nationality, who participated in the British Union of Fascists before defecting to Germany and taking German citizenship. A biography has been written by Mary Kenny, *Germany Calling: A Personal Biography of William Joyce, Lord Haw-Haw* (New Island 2008)
3. The bequest though continued to be a source of contention. As late as 1949 there were meetings with the solicitors of Leslie Howard's estate pleading for provision for Violette's needy parents. Also, by a codicil of 23 April 1943, Howard left a different property in Stoke Poges that he was in the process of buying to Josette Renée Paul Ronserail, a member of the Free French, with whom another relationship had developed. Josette had enlisted in the FANY (First Aid Nursing Yeomanry) and was recruited from there into the Special Operations Executive (SOE). She resigned from the FANY in December 1942. It was not clear what she did after that, but she married in September 1943.
4. See cabinet budget discussions in Colvin, *The Chamberlain Cabinet*.

Chapter 7

1. More commonly known as tungsten, but with chemical symbol W, Portugal had large deposits of wolframite ore at Panasqueira.
2. Predecessor of the modern Portela Airport, Lisbon.
3. A certificate issued to certify the cargo of a neutral ship so that it had assurance of passing through a blockade.
4. The Baron, however, felt no personal loyalty to either Hitler or the Nazi party. As a result of the treaty of friendship following the Molotov-

Ribbentrop pact in 1939, he had lost his castle in Lithuania and his aged mother was forced to move to another castle in Silesia without realising that that, in turn, had been confiscated from a Polish family. She died shortly afterwards.

5. The traffic of precious freight ran in both directions. Some of the Lufthansa crew were also Dutch, having been there when the Netherlands were occupied. Those on the route from Switzerland to Lisbon would bring in Swiss aviation instrumentation and wheel it across the runway at Portela for loading on to the BOAC flight which would then take the precious cargo to Britain for fitting in new aeroplanes. Source: conversation between Ben Rosevink and Bill Faro of KLM.

Chapter 8

1. Probably a reference to Walter Starkie, the British Council representative in Madrid. The description does not seem right for Tom Burns, the other noted intelligence operator there. It is possible that Starkie was the source of this bizarre tale, but it can also be noted that the General Officer Commanding for Gibraltar at the time was Mason MacFarlane, whom Colvin had known well in Berlin before the war, and who was similarly frustrated at the appeasement policies adopted by the British Government at the time, to the extent of involving himself with the visit of Ewald Kleist von Schmenzin to Britain in 1938.

Chapter 9

1. The bust has been identified as that of Margaret Maitland, née Lewis. She died in January 1942, a month after her son Lieutenant Thomas Maitland was killed in North Africa. She was a fine pianist and apparently often played with her eyes closed, which would be consistent with the pose in the bust.
2. More accurately 'had sat'. It must also have been one of the last portraits painted by Reginald Eves RA, since he died on 14 June 1941 – according to Royal Academy archives.
3. Howard did, however, execute a codicil leaving to Josette Renée Paule Ronserail a house he was buying in Stoke Poges, with a legacy in cash in case the purchase did not complete.
4. Its whereabouts are still unknown, as is that of Violette Cunnington. A solicitor's letter from Burgis & Co dated 1 September 1944 offered payment for the two busts.

5. Harold Spencer Jones 1890–1960. His visit was a little earlier and earned him a good conduct note from Walter Starkie of the British Council as that 'kind, modest scientist the Astronomer Royal', compared with the troublesome Howard.
6. Nom de plume derived from St Clement Danes for the novelist and playwright Winifred Ashton.

Chapter 10
1. The C-47 was the military derivative of the Douglas DC-3.
2. Who were they? According to the BOAC archives, wartime passenger lists were destroyed for security reasons. That was not the case for 1 June, but then the names had already been published in the newspapers. Without such records it is also difficult to ascertain whether it was that unusual to have only three passengers on a flight. If so, was there something of an extra risk in these passengers or the freight?

Chapter 11
1. Mrs Sharp had also persuaded her husband to negotiate with his employers the payment of a much higher life insurance policy than he had previously carried. Source: conversation with Ivan Sharp Jnr.

Chapter 12
1. The most likely author of this remark was Frank Foley, though Foley was a periodic visitor to the Lisbon embassy, rather than 'was in', working on a continuous basis.
2. Where Frank Foley had the daytime job of head of the Passport Office. His double life is described in Michael Smith's book, *Foley – The Spy Who Saved 10,000 Jews*.
3. Sir George Ogilvie-Forbes
4. Sir Harold Beeley KCMG CBE, 1909–2001, an academic who, in 1939, worked at Chatham House, then the Foreign Office Research Department. In 1946 he was Secretary of the Anglo-American Commission of Inquiry on Palestine. He was pessimistic about the effect of a possible foundation of a State of Israel on British influence in the Middle East. His career developed as an arabist diplomat.

Chapter 13
1. Chairman, British Council, 1942–45.
2. As Foreign Secretary, Anthony Eden played an instrumental part in persuading Howard to take in Madrid as well as Lisbon in his letter of 20

April. Among the concerns voiced by Howard about going to Spain was that his journey would be 'misinterpreted by the Russians'. Eden assured him that the Russians took 'a realistic view of Spanish affairs and of the importance of Spanish neutrality to the United Nations war effort'. Whether Howard took up Eden's invitation at the end of the letter to meet for dinner is not known.

3. Arthur Yencken was British Minister in Madrid. He had been in the Berlin Consulate before the war and reported on rearmament for MI6. He died in an air crash in Spain on 18 May 1944. Investigation showed this to have been an accident. An East German newssheet later alleged an assassination, but this was roundly refuted by Anthony Eden as Foreign Secretary (Hansard, 30 January 1953)

4. Before the war Blake was in the British Embassy in Prague. He helped Jewish refugees from the Sudetenland in camps in Czechoslovakia. After the war he became British Council representative in Portugal.

5. Sintra was no longer used for the flights as the new airport at Portela had opened on 15 October 1942.

6. The hotel was home for Calouste Gulbenkian during the war.

Chapter 14

1. Apparently a reference to Sir Samuel Hoare, the British Ambassador to Spain, who had gained the nickname from his handling of Indian affairs, then reinforced by his negotiation of the Hoare-Laval Pact.

2. The story of the Countess Miranda has to be seen as a composite. There were various women who crossed Howard's path in Madrid. One remarkable feature of Colvin's book is that Conchita Montenegro appears in a photograph with Leslie Howard during this trip, but is never mentioned in the text. Conchita Montenegro (1912–2007) was a Spanish dancer and actress who went to Hollywood. She co-starred with Howard in 'Never the Twain shall meet' (1931); despite the title, it seems there was an affair between them at the time. They certainly met again in Madrid. The second woman of note was Gloria von Fürstenberg, of Mexican origin, married to a German count (the second of her four husbands). Von Fürstenberg was renowned as one of the best-dressed women and indeed part of her wardrobe has found its way into the Victoria & Albert Museum. Howard spent much time talking with her and failed to be discreet about his travel plans, though, of course, these later changed. Thirdly there was a beautician at the Madrid Ritz, described by Burns as a German agent, of whom more later.

Chapter 15

1. Kearney had an evident interest in the world of cinema. He was on the jury of the Venice film festival from 1936 to 1939.
2. The theory of Howard as a special agent has been resurrected by Jose' Rey-Ximena in a book published in 2008. This resulted from conversations with Conchita Montenegro before her death, though previously she had been reluctant to give interviews. Montenegro was at the time engaged to Ricardo Giménez-Arnau, a prominent Falangist, who would have been able to secure a meeting with Franco. There was nothing new in such endeavours to win over Franco, and Sir Samuel Hoare was one of the main protagonists. Franco had anyway shown his Spanish capability to resist Hitler's blandishments at their meeting at Hendaye. Whether such a meeting took place is not clearly recorded, but it is unlikely that it would have had any momentous result. In practical terms, Howard had a heavy schedule in Madrid; the only possibility for meeting would be if his absences from the programme so assiduously prepared for him by Walter Starkie were actually just a ruse of nonchalance and forgetfulness.
3. In Eforgan's biography (p.225) this scene is recounted as an uncharacteristically strong clash, though at the end there is an understanding that Howard is not fit for the programme foisted upon him.
4. There is no clue as to the identity of this obliging cleric ready at short notice to round out the table numbers.
5. Howard's reluctance to fall in with the full British Council programme also led to some forceful criticism from him in a letter dated 28 May 1943 to W. Bridges-Adams, Deputy Director, Specialist Tours. Starkie had arranged repeat lectures to meet the demand for tickets, but Howard and Chenhalls had 'proceeded to take my typed programme and figuratively tear it to pieces'. Starkie complained that this was the only case of a visiting lecturer not keeping to the arrangements made for them. The tour was complicated by not being a purely Council affair, as Chenhalls, with Howard, was pursuing commercial film ventures, and Starkie found himself 'torn between rival claimants to his (Howard's) body!' On 2 June though, Starkie wrote again to Bridges-Adams in terms more appropriate in memoriam: 'In Spain there has been quite an extraordinary grief at his passing ... I wish I could convey to you the deep impression he made by his extraordinary reading of the Hamlet soliloquies. I shall never forget the performance, and it acquires all the deeper significance when one realises that it was his swan song.'

These letters were in the file that Howard's son Ronald was not allowed access to, and it remained closed till 1993.

6. Colvin draws a discreet veil at the end of the platform. Burns, in *Papa Spy*, has the beautician board the train with Howard to share a compartment, leaving the long-suffering Chenhalls to pass the night in the corridor. Eforgan cites the Baroness von Podewils as a Nazi underling in charge of the beauty salon. The full name was von Hese Mechthild Podewils-Dürniz.

Chapter 16

1. Harry Hopkins (1890–1946) was a close adviser to F. D. Roosevelt, urging priority against Germany in the war. He maintained relations with Churchill and Stalin, played an important role at Yalta and Potsdam and was the President's roving Lend-Lease ambassador.
2. The sorry state of the diminishing U-boat fleet is a factor to be considered when assessing the account given later by members of the former Luftwaffe crew. The introduction of the faster de Havilland Mosquito and the relative lack of submarines to protect had changed the nature of the Biscay theatre to concentrate more on aerial battles.
3. Nickname for US General Eisenhower, which later became the electoral slogan 'I like Ike'.

Chapter 17

1. Eforgan has a fuller account of this talented violinist who had taken refuge in Portugal.

Chapter 18

1. The English College, or Colegio dos Inglesinhos, was a long-established recusant college which continued to provide education until 1970. One boy who was there throughout the war confirms that he understood that Father Holmes, the acting head, needed to go to England on College business, but it is not clear that the sequence of events was as described here. See *The Lisbonian* 2006 & 2009, Monsignor Bill Dalton. Burns, p.263, has a different version: that a message was passed to Holmes, when he was already on the plane, that he was wanted urgently on the telephone, so he disembarked. Howard has the same account. There is no evidence that there actually was such a telephone call, simply that somebody was instructed to give him this message.

2. Who was the third person being booked on? As Father Holmes only had one seat, one or two more would still have to be sacrificed. Names of suggested other passengers bumped have included Squadron Leader Wally Lashbrook. But the reality was that, with the limited places and many priorities to be assessed, this and the waiting list were regular features of wartime civil aviation.
3. The questions remain whether these were the final lists, whether they were transmitted as a matter of routine and whether such transmission was likely to be translated into an immediate operational decision.

Chapter 19

1. The maximum passenger payload for a DC-3 was twenty-one. Ronald Howard records the *Ibis* as being one of those airliners fitted out with fourteen seats. That means that according to the manifest given to the Portuguese, there was one seat free. With only fourteen seats there would be more space for freight or luggage, though the limits to the plane's range may have restricted it to below the full payload.
2. Which would have been a compromising detail for a civilian flight. The suggestion though must have been made for Colvin to include this comment.
3. This concludes the account of the embarkation. It omits three alleged incidents which have come to light subsequently. First, Smith, recording an account by Patricia Dunstan, writes that Foley was booked on the flight. Maclean was not booked but had come to the airport and asked Foley to swap, saying that he wanted to get Howard's autograph. One would have thought there were easier ways to obtain an autograph. According to an article by Douglas L. Wheeler in the Association of Former Intelligence Officers' Periscope newsletter of 2005, Inspector General Maclean was misidentified by the Germans as a military general due possibly to a mistranslation of his title. If the account given to Patricia Dunstan were true, however, Maclean would not have been on the passenger list sent to Berlin on 31 May.

   Secondly Derek Partridge has a distinct memory of sitting as a young boy on the plane with his nanny, Dora Rove, when they were asked to give up their seats for two priority passengers. He saw the two boarding and recalls them as Howard and Chenhalls. There have been accounts of others too, George and William Cecil, sons of Cornelia Stuyvesant Vanderbilt, but these do not appear to have been properly substantiated.

Thirdly, contrary to Colvin's account, is the tale of Father Holmes who had apparently got to the plane before being passed a message that he was urgently required elsewhere, thus unwittingly reducing the complement of passengers to a fateful thirteen.

4. This lapse of time is in dispute – see Ch. 21.

5. This part of the account is based on a Luftwaffe report cited in Chapter 21. It is contested by various commentators, amongst other things contending that a civilian aircraft would not have parachute equipment. However, it is difficult to see why the German witnesses should have been false on this point. As Ronald Howard suggests, there came a stage when the aircraft was simply bursting apart, so anything or anybody could have come out. The inflatable life raft, then blazing, could have been confused for a parachute. Whatever it may have been, the observation by the German crews may have heightened the interest of the German command to return the next day to search.

Chapter 20

1. Secretary of State for Air and leader of the Liberal Party in the wartime coalition.

2. See www.n461.com/howard.html, edited by Rowan Matthews, for a discussion of the attacks on Flight 777 and the Sunderland N/461 (EJ134; UT-N, codenamed N for Nuts, of No. 461 Squadron, Royal Australian Air Force) the following day. Churchill had arrived in Gibraltar on 27 May from Washington. A new Avro York plane 'Ascalon' also arrived from England for his use. Incredibly, flying along the North African coast, it was to carry together Churchill, Eden, Ismay, Alexander, Alanbrooke, Tedder and Marshall. Quite a haul! The Sunderland captain, Flight Lieutenant Colin Walker, was interviewed by the BBC some days after. He confirmed that this was the day after the disappearance of Howard, that there were instructions to look for any surviving dinghy and that he believed the Germans were hunting every plane they could. This section of the interview was omitted from the broadcast.

   This same website reports that records relating to Howard's estate remain closed until January 2056. This is no longer true. The National Archives have now removed the embargo on the initiative of James Oglethorpe.

3. Confirmed by Derek Partridge when he took his delayed flight.

4. Ronald Howard, op. cit., devoted some research to the advanced radio tracking facilities installed by the Germans. As the Lisbon flights were

now operating under radio silence and were not visible, this was presumably an airborne radar type device which would still be able to track their route.

Chapter 21

1. This account by Friedlein was studied again many years later by Ben Rosevink, son of the lost radio operator from *Ibis*. Friedlein, by then an old man, substantially confirmed his earlier account, though he described it as a frontal attack, and made both by the planes of Bellstedt and Wittmer-Eigenbrodt; in that case, if true, it is difficult to see how there could have been a five-minute gap between observation and attack. It also conflicts directly with the radio message received from *Ibis*: 'unidentified aircraft follows me' – unless that message refers to a single plane outside the main Junkers formation.

   Ben Rosevink collaborated with Herbert Hintze, one of the pilots, in writing an article for *Flypast* of July 1993. Hintze explained why the patrol groups had grown to as many as eight; they had previously had little difficulty with some of the slower coastal planes and seaplanes of the RAF, but the newer generations of faster Mosquitoes (the de Havilland variety) had been inflicting heavy losses through their greater speed, and this called for a change of tactics in KG.40 squadrons. Defensively the Germans needed to fly higher so that they could attain greater velocity in a diving attack. This meant that they would be less adapted to submarine support work, but with the diminution of long-range Atlantic missions by U-boats, the emphasis in Biscay was more on aerial combat with the harrying Coastal Command. Strangely, Friedlein in his earlier interview with Colvin did not mention the Mosquitoes which had started to plague them. There is a revealing comment on relations in the command structure in the article by Hintze and Rosevink, after referring to the controversy raised by having attacked a civilian aircraft: We 'respected other flyers' (including the enemy crews) 'but we hated our bases, our staff and egg-headed COs. And we distrusted everybody whose military rank was higher than that of a captain.'

2. Bellstedt was in a position above the rest of the formation, so perhaps could have observed the target aircraft before Friedlein and others became aware of it. From that position he could also initiate dive into attack before ordering the others to follow (or Hintze ordering the others as the case may have been).

3. There are three different estimates for the lapse before attack, five minutes according to the Hemm report, straightaway according to Friedlein and nine minutes according to Colvin's source. The significance lies both in observation time to ascertain that it was not a plane of RAF Transport Command or another military user and in the possibility of communication to base for instructions, a theory promoted by R. Howard but without any direct evidence. It is interesting that Friedlein told Colvin: 'I'm not sure what instructions Lieutenant Bellstedt had when he attacked the airliner', which tacitly admits this possibility. There is a discrepancy in the versions after the attack between Friedlein – 'we did not stooge about' – the Hemm report, which did not give details of search activities, and Hintze's later recollection that after ordering a cease fire they 'scoured the area, but did not find' any remains on the sea.

4. According to Eforgan's enquiries, there was no Kowalewski as Commodore of KG.40. If so, it makes it difficult to evaluate his role in the story. Robert Kowalewski is not to be confused with Colonel Jan Kowalewski of the Polish General Staff who was posted by General Sikorski to Lisbon to work for the Free Poles and was instrumental in contacts with Canaris. A Lieutenant Colonel Robert Kowalewski was later squadron leader of KG.76 in attacks on Remagen bridge on the Rhine in March 1945 using new Arado jet planes. Could it be that Colvin was deliberately misled to keep Hemm at one remove from enquiries?

5. Hemm, commander of KG.40, was promoted to Major on 1 March 1943, and wrote the incident report, but the leader that day of the flight, according to Hintze, was not the squadron leader, Oblt Neccsany, but Hintze himself, co-author of the article with Rosevink. Colvin has no mention of Hintze (and one wonders how so many years later Hintze appears as squadron leader rather than Bellstedt), but does refer to Neccsany as pilot in the 'second pair'. The lists produced by Hintze on the other hand do not mention Neccsany as flying that day.

Chapter 22

1. G-AGBB was the only civilian passenger plane, but those days witnessed many attacks over the route that could have been taken by Churchill. Two Wellington bombers, a Douglas Boston and a Liberator were shot down in the Bay of Biscay area in the night of 1–2 June alone. The series of attacks ceased after Churchill's arrival in Britain.

2. According to Air Commodore John Mitchell, quoted in www.N461.com, whilst Churchill arrived from Washington in Gibraltar by Boeing Clipper,

the journey in North Africa and homeward was made by the Avro York Avalon. Churchill was not the only prime target; Air Commodore Mitchell writes that King George VI flew out on 11 June for a Victory Tour of Eighth Army, First Army and North African bases.

3. This account, oft repeated it seems in lectures on security, has led to recriminations concerning the speed of decoding and the question of responsibility for inaction. See also note to Ch. 19 *supra*. Some decoding was apparently more difficult in 1943 as the Enigma machines had been elaborated with additional rotors. Then if lists of passengers were being on occasion forwarded to Germany from the Lisbon embassy (other agents such as Kuno Weltzien, the local Krupp representative have also been suggested, but he was probably not operating effectively in May 1943), there is also the question of evaluating the significance of the communication on any particular occasion; a name does not necessarily mean a target.

Select Bibliography

Burns, Jimmy, *Papa Spy: Love, Faith and Betrayal in Wartime Spain* (London, Bloomsbury Publishing PLC, 2009) ISBN 978-0-7475-9520-5.

Churchill, Winston S., *The Hinge of Fate* (New York, Houghton-Mifflin, 1950)

Colvin Ian, *Admiral Canaris: Chief of Intelligence* (London, Gollancz, 1951)

Eforgan, Estel, *Leslie Howard: The Lost Actor* (London, Vallentine Mitchell Publishers, 2010) ISBN 978-0-85303-941-9

Goss, Chris, *Bloody Biscay: The Story of the Luftwaffe's Only Long Range Maritime Fighter Unit, V Gruppe / Kampfgeschwader 40, and Its Adversaries 1942–1944* (London: Crécy Publishing, 2001) ISBN 0-947554-87-4

Howard, Leslie Ruth, *A Quite Remarkable Father: A Biography of Leslie Howard* (New York: Harcourt Brace and Co., 1959)

Howard, Ronald, *In Search of My Father: A Portrait of Leslie Howard.* (London: St. Martin's Press, 1984) ISBN 0-312-41161-8

Rey Ximena, José, *El Vuolo de Ibis* [*The Flight of the Ibis*] (in Spanish). (Madrid: Facta Ediciones SL, 2008) ISBN 978-84-934875-1-5

Rosevink, Ben and Lt Col Herbert Hintze, 'Flight 777' *FlyPast*, Issue No. 120, July 1991

Shepherd, Naomi, *Wilfrid Israel – German Jewry's Secret Ambassador*, (London, Weidenfeld & Nicolson)

Southall, Ivan, *They Shall Not Pass Unseen* (London: Angus and Robertson, 1956)

Index